ROMAN DOMESTIC BUILDINGS

EXETER STUDIES IN HISTORY

General Editors:
Jonathan Barry, Tim Rees *and* T. P. Wiseman

Other paperbacks in this series include:

Roman Political Life, 90 BC–AD *69*
edited by T. P. Wiseman (1985)

The Administration of the Roman Empire, 241 BC–AD *193*
edited by David Braund (1988)

Satire and Society in Ancient Rome
edited by Susan H. Braund (1989)

Flavius Josephus: Death of an Emperor
translated with an introduction and commentary
by T. P. Wiseman (1991)

Historiography and Imagination: Eight Essays on Roman Culture
by T. P. Wiseman (1994)

Roman Public Buildings
edited by Ian M. Barton (new edition 1995)

ROMAN DOMESTIC BUILDINGS

Edited by
Ian M. Barton

UNIVERSITY
of
EXETER
PRESS

First published in 1996 by
University of Exeter Press
Reed Hall, Streatham Drive
Exeter EX4 4QR
UK
www.exeterpress.co.uk

Reprinted 2003, 2008

British Library Cataloguing in Publication Data
A catalogue record for this book is available
from the British Library

ISBN 978 0 85989 415 9

Typeset in 10/12 Sabon
by Exe Valley Dataset Ltd, Exeter

Printed and bound in Great Britain
by Short Run Press Ltd, Exeter

Contents

Figures, Plates and Maps

An Index of sites and buildings mentioned in the text, is included at the end of this book. This Index is supplemented by several maps locating each site in its geographical context.

I. Figures

II. Plates *(located between pp. 80 and 81)*

Acknowledgements

Once again I have to thank the Editorial Committee of the Exeter Studies in History series for commissioning this sequel to *Roman Public Buildings*, which was published in that series in 1989, and I apologize to them and to my fellow-contributors for the long delay in publication. I owe special thanks to the latter for their contributions and for their willingness to humour my editorial whims; and amongst them I must make particular mention of Tony Brothers for his helpful criticisms of my own material. I also wish to thank Peter Wiseman for his encouragement and help. I am grateful to Simon Baker, the Secretary of University of Exeter Press, and his staff for their patience and help; also to the History and Archaeology Drawing Office at Exeter University for drawing the plan of the Vindolanda 'palace' and to Trevor Harris and Stephen Dodd at Lampeter for the maps and the plan of the 'Libraries' terrace at Hadrian's Villa, and to Geraint Davies for photographic work. I acknowledge with gratitude a generous grant from the Pantyfedwen Trust of University of Wales, Lampeter, towards the cost of the illustrations. Several scholars gave valuable advice to me and to other contributors, and their help is acknowledged in the notes; but I must make special mention here of Robin Birley, who on two occasions made me welcome at Vindolanda and showed me something of his excavations and their results, and of David Breeze, who generously sent a revised plan and reconstruction of the Barburgh Mill fortlet.

The following have kindly given permission for the reproduction of copyright material:

Figures

R. Agache: 29; B.T. Batsford Ltd and Frank Sear: 36; Robin Birley: 40; de Boccard Édition-Diffusion: 24; The British School at Rome: 22, 23; Cadw: Welsh Historic Monuments: 7; Amanda Claridge: 14; Croom Helm: 8, 10; Cumberland and Westmorland Antiquarian and Archaeological Society: 63; David Breeze and Michael Moore: 58; Éditions du CNRS: 30; J.M. Dent and Sons Ltd: 5; English Heritage and Kent Archaeological Society: 25; K. Gleason and E. Netzer: 52; Dr W.S. Hanson: 62(b); HarperCollins Publishers: 28; Christina Häuber: 46; The Johns Hopkins University Press: 3, 21; Istituto Poligrafico e Zecca dello Stato: 9; Wilhelmina Jashemski: 43, 53; Guide archeologiche Laterza: 38, 55; Methuen London: 33, 34, 35; D.S. Neal: 26; Prof. Dr H.U. Nuber: 61, 62(d); Oxford University Press: 18, 19, 20; T.W. Potter: 4; Prof. F. Rakob: 48, 49; Römisch-Germanische Kommission: 65, 68; Society for the Promotion of Roman Studies: 56, 60(b); Society of Antiquaries of Scotland: 57, 62(a); Swan Hellenic: 41; Bryan Ward-Perkins and the Editor of *Antiquity*: 32; Weidenfeld and Nicolson Ltd: 12, 13, 17; Prof. R.J.A. Wilson: 42, 64; Yale University Press: 15, 16; and William L. MacDonald: 37; Philipp von Zabern: 31, 50.

Plates

A.M. 716 (Rome): 1, 15; Ian Barton: 3, 14, 16, 18, 19, 20, 22; Brian Brake: 2; Tony Brothers: 7–13 inclusive, 21; David Davison: 24–30 inclusive; Soprintendenza Archeologica di Roma: 23; Eddie Owens: 4, 5, 6; Yale University Press and William L. MacDonald: 17.

To all of the above I am extremely grateful, and I apologize for any errors of attribution. If any copyright holder has been inadvertently omitted, we shall gladly correct the omission in any reprint.

Notes on Contributors

Ian M. Barton read Classics at Corpus Christi College, Cambridge, and after lecturing at Keele and in Ghana went to Saint David's University College, Lampeter, where he taught for thirty years until his retirement, and was for some years Head of the Department of Classics. His special interests include classical art and architecture and Roman imperial history, especially that of North Africa. He is the author of *Africa in the Roman Empire,* and edited *Roman Public Buildings* in this series.

A.J. Brothers, a graduate of The Queen's College, Oxford, is Senior Lecturer in the Department of Classics at University of Wales, Lampeter (formerly Saint David's University College), where his lecturing commitments include Greek and Roman architecture. His chief research interest is Roman comedy (particularly Terence), but he has also published articles on Roman architecture and religion. He frequently acts as lecturer and guide at classical sites around the Mediterranean.

David P. Davison was educated at The King's School, Canterbury and Westfield College, University of London, and took his DPhil at Worcester College, Oxford; his doctoral thesis was on the Barracks of the Roman Army from the 1st to 3rd Centuries AD. He has also studied at the Johannes Gutenberg-Universität, Mainz. His special interest is in the north-west provinces of the Roman Empire, where he has travelled and excavated widely. He is now Principal Director of Tempvs Reparatvm Archaeological and Historical Associates Limited, and General Editor of British Archaeological Reports (BAR).

E.J. Owens was educated at Liverpool Collegiate School and Sheffield University, where he undertook research for M.A. and PhD. He was a Junior Research Fellow at Sheffield before taking up his present appointment at University of Wales, Swansea, in 1978. His main interests lie in Roman Republican history and Graeco-Roman archaeology, and his book *The City in the Greek and Roman World* was published in 1991.

John Percival is Professor of Ancient History and Head of the School of History and Archaeology at University of Wales, Cardiff. His specialist area of research is the social and economic history of the later Roman Empire, and he has published *The Reign of Charlemagne* (with H.R. Loyn, 1975), *The Roman Villa: an Historical Introduction* (1976; 2nd edition 1988), and numerous papers on associated topics. He is currently working on the role of villas and villa ruins in fifth- and sixth-century Gaul, and is co-editor of a forthcoming *Dictionary of the Peoples of Europe*.

Nicholas Purcell is a Fellow of St John's College, Oxford, where he has been Tutor in Ancient History since 1979. He is also a University Lecturer (C.U.F.) in Ancient History. He has a special interest in the archaeology and social history of Roman Italy, and has made detailed studies of the relation between gardens, architecture and landscape.

Abbreviations for Collections of Inscriptions

CIL   Corpus Inscriptionum Latinarum

OGIS   Orientis Graeci Inscriptiones Selectae

RIB   Roman Inscriptions of Britain

SIG   Sylloge Inscriptionum Graecarum

Introduction

IAN M. BARTON

In the introduction to a previous volume of this series, on Roman public buildings, I expressed the hope that an opportunity might be afforded to complete the 'rounded architectural picture' of Roman society by adding a volume on domestic buildings 'from the hovels of peasants to the palaces of monarchs'. Here is that volume. It must be admitted that not much will be found in the pages that follow about the hovels of peasants; but I hope we have managed to do justice to most types of residential accommodation at different levels of the social scale. As in *Roman Public Buildings*, we begin with a chapter on town planning, this time with particular reference to the planning of residential areas. The next two chapters deal respectively with houses in towns and houses in the country, and then there is a chapter which looks in detail at the development of imperial palaces. An integral part of nearly every house above the most basic level is its garden, so the next chapter discusses gardens as a part of domestic architecture. Finally there is a separate study of the residential accommodation provided for soldiers of the Roman army in legionary fortresses and auxiliary forts.

It will be seen from this brief summary that the range of structures included under the term 'domestic buildings' is vast. Indeed, it could be argued that some of them could equally be regarded as 'public buildings'; this would certainly apply to the official residences of the emperors, and perhaps also to the military accommodation, inasmuch as that was state property. Roman society made a less sharp distinction than ours generally does between the public and private spheres, and at least among the upper classes the house was as much a place of official business as a private family residence—so that when Augustus became *princeps,* the development of his house into a palace was a natural extension of what Republican nobles' houses had always been. Perhaps the nearest parallel in modern Britain would be the dual function of residence and workplace allotted to such houses as 10 Downing Street or Lambeth Palace.

There is less evidence about residential buildings to be gleaned from theoretical writings than there was in the case of public buildings. Vitruvius was clearly more interested in public architecture, though he does devote Book VI of his work on architecture to domestic buildings. However, much even of this book is devoted to generalities; but his treatment of the planning of different types of house is of much interest, though perhaps it hardly does justice to the great variety of types which actually existed. Writers of agricultural textbooks like Cato and Varro convey a certain amount of information about villas; but more useful are literary descriptions of particular houses, notably those which the younger Pliny gives in his *Letters.* Naturally, such descriptions only tell us about the houses of the rich.

The archaeological record too tends to favour the dwellings of wealthier citizens, especially as the earlier excavators were more interested in treasure hunting than in recording the social aspects of the places they were investigating; hence the gaps in the decorative schemes of some houses in Herculaneum and Pompeii. (In modern times, of course, it is the activities of illicit treasure-hunters that have caused the disappearance from their context of such decorative features as the *oscilli* in some of the peristyle gardens.) Even now the dominant feature of the picture conjured up in most people's minds by the word *villa* is probably the figured mosaic pavement, though such luxury items were only to be found in a minority of the dwellings to which that term could be applied. Inevitably, therefore, our survey (except in the military chapter) will be skewed in the direction of the lifestyle of the more prosperous members of society. Nevertheless, it may be remembered that the urban and rural establishments of senators and members of the equestrian order, and in the provinces of the *decuriones,* the men who made up the local councils of the municipalities, provided employment and accommodation for many lesser folk, especially slaves and freed-men; indeed a magnate's slaves in his town or country mansion probably lived more comfortably than most free citizens. The complaints of Juvenal's friend Umbricius in the *Third Satire* may not be over-much exaggerated.

At this point it may be as well to say something about the technical terms applied to different types of residential accommodation. The basic Latin word for 'house' is *aedes* (plural—the singular means 'temple'), from which are formed the verb *aedificare* (build) and the noun *aedificium*, which means any type of 'building'. The word which corres-ponds to our 'home'—a family's dwelling—is *domus*, and by the first century B.C. this word had come to be used in particular to denote a self-contained town house as opposed to either a country house (*villa*) or a cottage or hovel (*casa*);[1] so it is the appropriate word for the houses at Pompeii and Herculaneum described in Chapter 2. By that time also, at least in the capital, shortage of land and the need to accommodate an increasing population had begun to lead to the construction of tenement blocks rising to several storeys. The word *insulae* (islands) is already used for such structures by Cicero, writing in the 40s B.C. about an incident which had taken place half a century before,[2] and in the early second century A.D. Tacitus and Suetonius both specifically distinguish the *insula* from the *domus* or, as it is elsewhere called, the private house (*privatae aedes*).[3] The use of this term, however, can be confusing, because modern writers—apparently without any ancient authority—use the same word to denote what in America is called a 'block', i.e. an area in a town enclosed by streets on all four sides. This use of the word is so well established that it would be pedantic to object to it, and it is so used in our Chapter 1; but this does mean that when the discussion passes to tenement blocks, as it does on pp. 23f, the word will be used with a change of meaning: you are hereby warned!

An additional source of information for the city of Rome is the Marble Plan (*Forma Urbis*) which was put up early in the third century A.D. by the orders of Septimius Severus in Vespasian's Temple of Peace, where it apparently superseded an earlier version.[4] Although the plan is extant only in fragments, several of these are extensive enough to give a clear impression of the layout of various areas of the city. From these can be seen how those parts which had been devastated by the fire of A.D. 64 were re-planned on orthogonal lines, as well as the extent to which *insulae*, often adjoining commercial premises, had replaced *domus* as the predominant residential type (fig. 1).

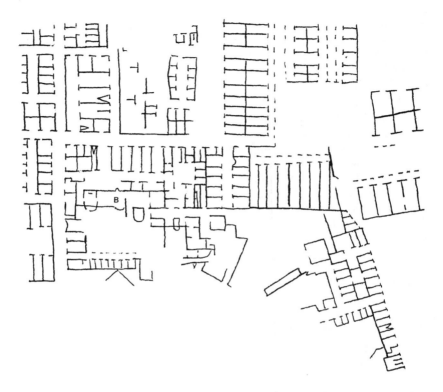

Fig. 1: Sketch of part of the Marble Plan of the City of Rome (*Forma Urbis*). It shows an area in Trastevere where two different alignments are juxtaposed. The buildings include numerous shops and other commercial premises, as well as a bath building (B) and apartment houses (*insulae*), indicated by the V-shaped symbols, which represent staircases.

Readers may find in this book a greater concentration on Italy than in *Roman Public Buildings*, particularly where houses in towns are concerned. This is in part necessitated by the nature of the archaeological evidence; the excavation of the buried cities of Pompeii and Herculaneum and the almost complete recovery of the town plan of Ostia make it inevitable that the majority of our examples of town houses will be drawn from these sites. In any case, Italy to a large extent set a norm for the Empire as a whole, especially the western provinces, so it may not be too misleading to concentrate on its domestic architecture. Besides the Italian sites and the others discussed (many of them, especially country houses, in Gaul and Britain), there are many others which could have been cited—from north Africa, for example, town houses at Utica, Thugga or Sabratha, or country houses from the fertile coastal area of Tripolitania. And exciting new finds continue to be made; in this book examples will be found of recent discoveries from opposite ends of the Empire: the 'palace' at Vindolanda near Hadrian's Wall (p. 112) and the garden at Herod the Great's villa near Jericho (p. 141). Even in Rome itself the archaeologists can still surprise us. Excavations in the Forum have recently provided possible confirmation of a statement by Suetonius about Caligula's palace which had always been regarded as pure exaggeration (p. 94). For almost every example included in this book, probably half a dozen more could be adduced from different parts of the Roman world; we have aimed to present a representative sample rather than a complete register.

NOTES

1. Vitruvius 2.1.7.

2. Cicero, *de Officiis* 3.66: Cato's father (who died before 91 B.C.) was judge in a case which turned on a new *insula* blocking the view of the augurs from the Capitol hill.

3. Tacitus, *Annals* 6.45; 15.41; Suetonius, *Nero* 16.1; 38.2 (*domus*); 44.2 (*privatae aedes*).

4. G. Carettoni et al., *La Pianta marmorea di Roma antica* (2 vols, Rome 1960), supplemented by E. Rodriguez-Almeida, *Forma urbis marmorea: aggiornamento generale 1980* (Rome 1981).

1

Residential Districts

E. J. Owens

The city was a complex structure in which public, private and sacred demands for space had to be accommodated. In many of the native towns of Italy, like their counterparts in the Aegean, there was little or no formal organisation of space. Towns grew without order. Livy's description of the rebuilding of Rome after the sack of the city by the Gauls in 390 B.C. emphasises the continued irregularity of the city. As Livy's account reveals, there was no attempt to replan after the departure of the Gauls.[1] The damaged houses and buildings were simply reconstructed on their original plots, and, subsequently, the residential areas continued to expand. The result was confusion (pl. 1). The reasons why the Romans did not take the opportunity to replan their city are more complex than the haste to which Livy refers in his account. Several factors contributed to the decision not to replan. In the first place, it is apparent from the evidence that the destruction of the city was nowhere as complete as Livy implies. In consequence, in many cases houses could be rebuilt on their original foundations. Secondly, the personal interests of the property owners were involved in the decision. Thirdly, the replanning of the city, involving any radical redistribution of land, might have had a serious impact on the social and even the political structures of ancient Rome. Thus, the scope for a radical replanning of Rome was limited, and private housing continued to spread without order.

In describing the fire of 210 B.C. Livy offers a graphic description of the area around the Roman Forum before the construction of the basilicas and other public buildings, which later flanked the public square.[2] Private houses crowded around the shops which faced on to the Forum at the time. Consequently, when the fire broke out, it spread rapidly, destroying not only domestic buildings but also the fish market, the house of the Vestals and an area known as the Quarries which, at least by the time of Cato the Elder, also contained residential occupation. The fire even threatened to engulf the shrine of Vesta some distance to the south. Livy's description of the fire and the area which it destroyed reveals that the district around the Forum was a confusion of private, commercial, sacred and public buildings. The close proximity of one building to another assisted the spread of the fire, which burned uncontrollably night and day.

The fire of 210 B.C. was just one of many fires which damaged the city of Rome during Republican and early Imperial times. Yet it was not until the great fire of A.D. 64, which destroyed a large part of Rome, that an attempt was made to transform the city through the efforts of the emperor Nero. Whilst the surviving accounts of Nero's measures are by no means complete, they reveal the importance placed by the emperor on improving the residential areas of the city. These areas had suffered particularly badly as a result of the fire[3] and, as in the earlier fire of 210 B.C., the overcrowded living conditions had been one of the chief causes for its initial spread. The areas destroyed by the fire were replanned (fig. 1). The streets were widened and the frontages of the buildings were regulated, and had to be protected by colonnades. Building and fire regulations were also improved. A fixed proportion of buildings had to be constructed from stone and maximum heights to buildings were established. Householders had to provide fire-fighting apparatus. Furthermore, to reduce the risk of fires spreading rapidly from building to building, party walls were forbidden, and buildings had to have their own independent walls.[4]

The living conditions of ancient Rome reflected on a larger scale conditions in native cities throughout Italy. Domestic quarters grew haphazardly, without order or regulation. Houses and other buildings crowded together, often producing cramped, overcrowded conditions and the typical sinuous, narrow streets. Even within the domestic quarters, the houses themselves show little regularity. Often they were fitted into any available space and were altered opportunistically as more space became available. Initially, houses tended to concentrate along the main roadways and around the designated civic areas of the town; and then later they slowly spread out to the less accessible or desirable areas. Evidence from Veii before its destruction by the Romans in 396 B.C. indicates that this major Etruscan centre was evolving in this way. Except for a small residential area on the citadel of Piazza d'Armi, which shows some signs of regularity, the houses, shops and other buildings of the early town spread without order, initially along the main routes of communication, which ran through the site, and around the public buildings.

The haphazard irregularity of the native towns of northern and central Italy contrasts markedly with the Greek colonies of southern Italy and Sicily. The contrast is illustrated by Cicero's comparison of the

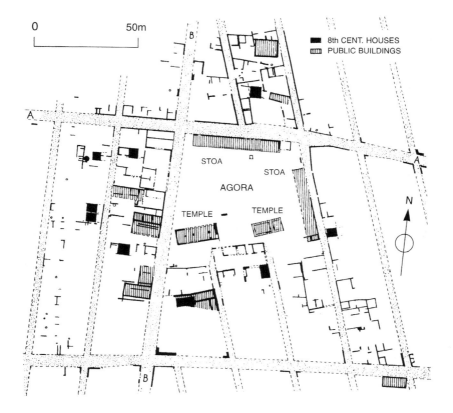

Fig. 2: Megara Hyblaea: plan of the Greek colony, sixth century B.C.

hill-towns of Latium with the spacious, well laid-out cities of Campania, which had developed under Greek influence.[5] In colonising the fertile coastal regions of southern Italy and Sicily, the Greek settlers had been faced with the problems of establishing new *poleis* where none had existed before. The formula adopted, based on the division of land into public, private and sacred use, was simple but effective, and reflected the three main elements which comprised the ancient city.

The system is admirably illustrated at Megara Hyblaea (fig. 2). The colony was established on the east coast of Sicily in the second half of the eighth century B.C., and throughout the seventh and sixth centuries the town prospered. The town plan, apparently laid out at the initial foundation of the colony, allocated sites for temples, the agora, which later had to be increased in size at the expense of the surrounding residential *insulae*, and the lines of the major streets. Much of the space within the town was allocated to residential occupation. The residential areas, with differing orientations, were organised in a series of irregular shaped, elongated rectangles. Each *insula* was divided longitudinally into two strips by a wall and was clearly demarcated from the public streets by low stone curbs.

Initially within the residential *insulae* private development was fairly unrestrained. The small eighth-century houses usually faced the streets but were often not contiguous. Moreover, the individual house plots were not of equal size. The difference in size of the building plots suggests some form of social hierarchy within the early population. Possibly this was based on differences in status between the original colonists and later additions to the population. Such a distinction between the original colonists and later settlers is clearly evidenced at Black Kerkyra (Corcyra Nigra, Korčula). Here, a fourth-century inscription records the difference in landowning rights between the initial colonists and the later arrivals.[6] On the other hand, the discrepancies in the size of properties at Megara Hyblaea and other early colonies might also reflect the established social and political hierarchy of pre-Classical society in general.

As Megara Hyblaea prospered, so new residential districts were added, and the houses were renovated and enlarged. Nevertheless, the overall division of the residential quarters into elongated strips was maintained. The division of residential areas into a series of elongated, rectangular *insulae* was the common feature of regularly planned towns throughout the Greek world. The arrangement of the houses within the house blocks was also often standardised.

The northern hill of Olynthos, a city chosen in c.432 B.C. as the capital of the Chalcidic League, offers a unique glimpse of the domestic quarters of a city in the Classical period (fig. 3). Excavations by archaeologists from Johns Hopkins University uncovered a large area of the domestic districts of Olynthos. The hill was divided by a grid of intersecting streets into regular, elongated rectangular building blocks. Each block was divided longitudinally into two strips, and each strip usually contained a row of five adjacent houses. Even the houses themselves were standard. Each usually contained a row of adjacent rooms facing south, through a deep portico, on to the courtyard.

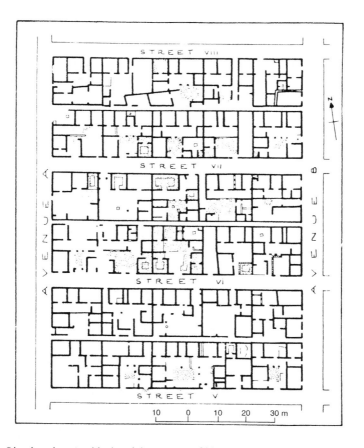

Fig. 3: Olynthos: housing blocks of the new city, fifth century B.C.

By the fifth century B.C. the domestic quarters of many of the Greek towns in the west followed a similar arrangement. For instance at Himera in Sicily the residential *insulae* of the fifth-century town were subdivided into two rows of houses of equal size. Unlike at Olynthos, however, the houses at Himera were bounded on three sides by narrow alleyways and, thus, were completely free-standing. Such an arrangement obviated party walls and potential boundary disputes between neighbours, and presumably also assisted drainage. Obviously such uniformity of construction within the domestic quarters of a city was facilitated by the level topography of the site. Equally important in promoting uniformity, however, was the spread of democracy and its emphasis on the equality of all citizens.

When the Romans began the process of colonisation in Italy, equality of ownership was central to land distribution within the settlements. Cosa (Ansedonia) provides a clear example (fig. 4). The city was established in 273 B.C. as one of a pair of colonies on the coast of the Tyrrhenian Sea 139 km to the north-west of Rome. Over the following two centuries the city prospered, until it was sacked in the 60s B.C. Although it was partially rebuilt during the principate of Augustus and remained a local cult centre until the middle of the third century A.D., it never regained its former importance.

Its plan reflects the adaptation of Greek planning experience in Italy to the needs of a Roman colony. The irregular perimeter was heavily fortified with massive polygonal walls. The southern corner was demarcated by a wall and reserved as the *arx*, whilst the small forum was situated close to the south-eastern gate, through which the road to the harbour passed. Although there were other public buildings in different parts of the town, most of the area within the walls was given over to residential occupation.

The residential blocks were rectangular in shape and where necessary were terraced. Excavations within the domestic quarters of the city have revealed that each residential block was divided by a wall along its longitudinal axis into two parallel rows of houses. Each house in turn opened on to one of the streets, which ran between the successive *insulae*. In the original settlement house plots were of uniform size and had generally standardised internal arrangements. Such uniformity resulted from the theoretical concept that all of the colonists were equal, and that, consequently, each colonist should be given an equal distribution of land both within the urban area and in the territory outside the colony.

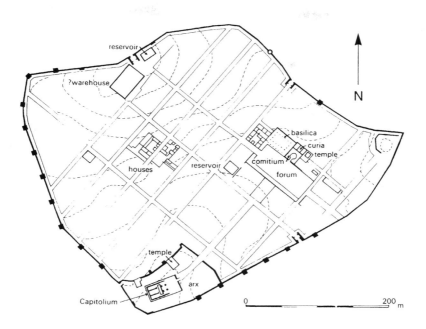

Fig. 4: Cosa: plan of the Roman colony laid out in the third century B.C. (contour intervals 4 m). Most of the blocks not occupied by public buildings appear to have contained houses.

Equality of ownership, however, could not be maintained over a long period of time. Subsequent levels within the housing blocks reveal that houses changed, increasing or diminishing in size at the expense of neighbouring plots. These changes undoubtedly reflect the changing fortunes of the owners. Some families prospered, whilst others moved away or died off.

As Cosa and other early colonies reveal, Roman colonial planning was inspired by Greek experience, but it was not merely a copy. In conquering northern Italy the Romans developed a distinctive urban design, which was suited to their colonial needs. The layout, with numerous variations, eventually became the standard layout of Roman cities throughout the Empire. The design was characterised by two intersecting major roadways. The consequent street grid produced characteristically square or slightly oblong residential blocks. The colonies were overtly military, and their overall layout and construction emphasised the military needs of the settlement. However, the shape and often the uniform size of the *insulae*, regularly measuring 75–80 m square, clearly suggests the influence of land surveying in the layout of the towns.

The typically square or sub-square blocks formed the basis of the residential quarters in new cities throughout the Empire. Unfortunately, because of continuous occupation from antiquity, in many cases it is impossible to gain a clear picture of the internal arrangements of the properties within such housing blocks. Indeed, the internal arrangements of the *insulae* must have varied considerably depending upon the size of the population, the type of housing involved, and the level of urbanisation attained. Despite these difficulties, some cities still reveal indications of the internal arrangements of the *insulae*. At Verona, for example, the alignment of the courtyards of modern houses suggests that the *insulae*, which are reflected in the modern street system, were regularly subdivided by narrower streets.[7] Excavations at Calleva Atrebatum (Silchester) revealed the existence of narrow, sometimes metalled, lanes, which provided access to the properties inside the residential housing blocks, although, in contrast to the arrangements at Verona, the internal divisions show little regularity.[8]

Calleva, the capital of the Atrebates, was laid out as a series of approximately square or slightly oblong *insulae* (fig. 5). However, despite its role as a *civitas* capital, the urban population remained relatively small and the residential *insulae* were never completely built up. The number, orientation and type of buildings within each housing block varied. Even in the most built-up of the residential blocks few buildings were contiguous. Often there is much free space, which is either unused or given over to gardens and other forms of cultivated plots. The houses and other buildings within the plots vary in size, orientation and grandeur. As elsewhere, they were altered and renovated in response to the changing conditions and fortunes of the occupants. Although Calleva was an important regional centre, the impression which remains is that of a pleasant, spacious market town, which developed slowly in response to the growing acceptance of urban life by the Atrebates.

The internal configuration of the *insulae* at Calleva Atrebatum can be contrasted with that of the Roman colony of Thamugadi (Timgad) in north Africa (fig. 6). Thamugadi was planted in the early years of Trajan's reign by the legate of the Third Legion Augusta, which was stationed at Lambaesis. Its layout is stark and rigid. The residential districts of the colony were divided by the street system into small *insulae* approximately 20 m square, although it is possible that the preserved house blocks were, in fact, subdivisions of the larger *insula*, typical of Roman colonies, which measured 75–80 m square. Occupation density was high. Each block was fully developed and was divided by walls into two or three house plots (pl. 2). The rigidity of Timgad's

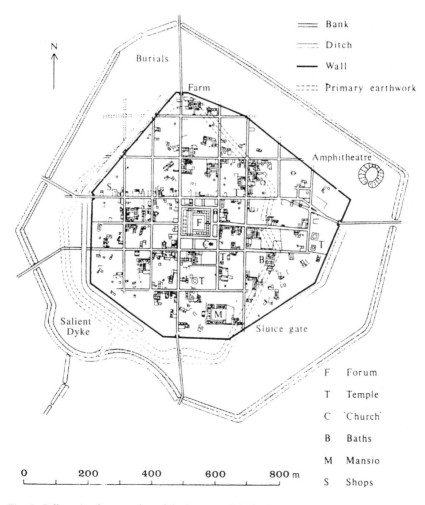

Fig. 5: Calleva Atrebatum: plan of the Romano-British city.

layout, however, is somewhat exceptional and was even abandoned as the city later expanded.

Although areas of a city were specifically laid out as domestic quarters, shops, commercial properties, and even public buildings were to be found in an often complex relationship with the houses.[9] The economic potential of residential quarters is witnessed by the appearance of shops, industrial establishments and other commercial properties as part of residential *insulae*. Suetonius tells how Nero accused Salvidienus Orfitus of renting out three shops, which formed part of his private

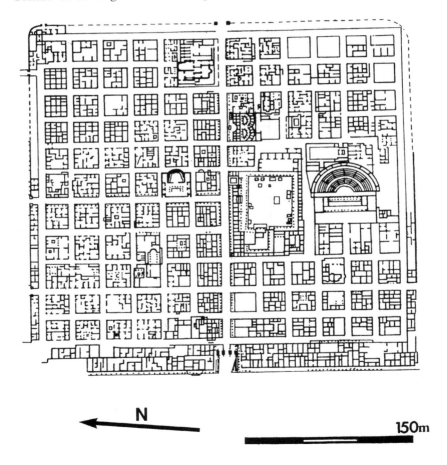

N   150m

Fig. 6: Thamugadi: plan of the Roman veteran colony.

house, as offices to foreign states.[10] Such establishments were usually located along the major roads, where trade and the incentive for profit were greatest, but they might also be found throughout the residential quarters. Not only were the outlets for finished goods to be found in domestic quarters, but also the small manufacturing establishments, with furnaces and other indications of industrial activity, which produced the goods and commodities. Evidence of the interaction of commercial activity with domestic accommodation can be found as early as the Etruscan colony of Marzabotto, which was established on the flood plain of the River Reno, a tributary of the River Po. The town was planted towards the end of the sixth century B.C. and an early feature of its development was the inclusion of shops and other commercial properties along the streets.[11]

Similarly, essential public amenities were not necessarily confined to public areas of a city. The evidence from cities as far apart as Timgad, Silchester and Pompeii reveals the presence of such large public buildings as bath houses within the residential areas, where they could be most accessible to the inhabitants. Temples were another type of public building which were not necessarily confined to specifically civic or sacred areas. Small temples could be found throughout the domestic quarters. At Silchester several temples were found in the residential quarters of the city, and it seems certain that in some cases the temples were associated with local guilds.[12]

Status and social position were a central part of life in the Roman world and were conveyed by dress and other visible signs.[13] Nevertheless, there is little evidence of the elitist segregation of domestic quarters. Occasionally, the houses of the aristocracy might group in a particular area of the city. For instance, the Palatine hill attracted the residences of the wealthier citizens of Rome, and its exclusiveness continued throughout the history of the city, especially after it became the place of residence of the emperor.[14] But the Palatine was exceptional (cf. Chapter 4 below).

Indeed the nexus of Roman social and political relations often promoted the opposite tendency, namely the admixture of the properties of the rich and the poor. It is a well-known fact that Caesar's first house was a modest dwelling which was located in the less salubrious Subura district of Rome.[15] Similarly, Pompey owned property in the Carinae district of Rome.[16] Sometimes even a political statement could be made by the location at which a public figure bought a house. On his return from Africa, Gaius Gracchus, in keeping with his democratic principles, abandoned his house on the Palatine and bought another close to the Forum.[17] In the same way, when Marius returned from Asia, he chose to have a house built close to the Forum in order to maintain his popularity.[18]

It was not the desire to live apart from their fellow-citizens which dictated where the houses of the rich were located. It was, rather, the physical aspect of the location which was attractive. For example, either the top or the upper slopes of a hill were often favoured. Such a location not only offered the benefit of cooling breezes in the summer, but could also act as a virtual podium, on which the house was placed, in order that it might be seen by all. Thus, Cicero boasted that his house on the Palatine was eminently positioned so as to be seen, and presumably recognised as his, by his fellow-citizens.[19]

The integration of the elite houses with the shops and residences of the commoners is a regular feature of the cities of the Empire. At Athens in the Roman period two spacious courtyard houses were constructed in the valley between the Areopagus and the Pnyx, which was otherwise crowded with small, mean houses and workshops.[20] At the other end of the Roman world, Venta Silurum (Caerwent), the tribal capital and administrative centre of the Silures of south Wales, offers similar evidence for the admixture of properties of different types belonging to owners of differing status (fig. 7). Although here, as elsewhere, there is evidence of free space such as gardens and orchards within the town, in general the houses, shops and other buildings were more densely packed than at Silchester. In the excavated *insulae* narrow strip houses and shops crowded along the streets. The buildings were long and narrow, and some at least revealed additions to the rear, suggesting differing prosperity between owners.

Despite the demand for space, narrow alleys, for access to the properties in the interiors of the *insulae*, and to assist drainage, separated many of the strip houses/shops. Larger courtyard houses were located behind the strip buildings.[21] One example of the relationship between properties of different kinds is found in the *insula* immediately to the west of the forum. Here a large courtyard house was positioned behind a row of strip dwellings and shops, which fronted on to one of the main north-south streets of the town. The location of a spacious courtyard house in the interior of the *insula* suggests that, although the owner of the courtyard house might have wanted a certain amount of seclusion and privacy, at the same time he desired to remain closely associated with the urban commoners and their economic activities. Similar observations can be made about the domestic quarters of towns throughout the Empire.

In many cases the archaeological exploration of the domestic quarters of a town has been sporadic. This may be because of lack of funds, the interests of the excavators, or the fact that continuous occupation of the town from antiquity precludes widespread excavation. Fortunately Pompeii, Herculaneum and Rome's harbour town of Ostia offer detailed evidence of the influences which conditioned the development and the arrangement of domestic areas. They also allow comparison between the arrangements of a harbour town and the nature of small urban centres in Campania.

The original native Oscan settlement of Pompeii was confined to the south-western corner of the later enlarged town, which eventually

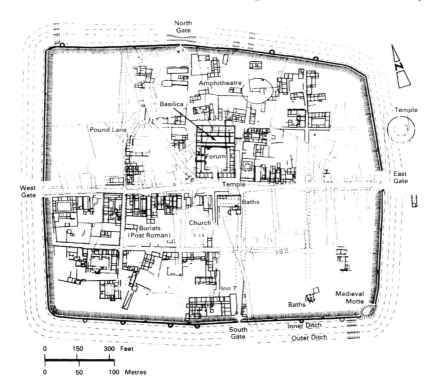

Fig. 7: Venta Silurum: plan of the Romano-British city. The Pound Lane site (p. 60) is between Pound Lane and the main east-west street.

covered an area of approximately 65 ha. As the town expanded, a series
of approximately rectangular extensions was added. The overall plan of
the enlarged town was based on the intersection of two main east–west
roads with one major north–south road (fig. 8). The major public areas
concentrated around the old Oscan centre, the triangular forum, and the
palaestra and amphitheatre in the extreme south-eastern corner. The rest
of the area enclosed by the walls was given over to residential occupation (pl. 3). Although the overall plan of the residential districts was
rectangular, there was much variation within the individual districts. The
residential *insulae* of the different regions often varied in size, shape,
orientation and internal configuration. Moreover, the layout and organisation of the residential districts and the integration of the buildings of
different types reveals a complexity of relationships, which reflects the
complexity of urban life.

First, the interdependence between a town and its surrounding
territory in the ancient world is unquestioned. One aspect of this
relationship, already mentioned above (p. 14), was the use of land-
surveying techniques in the laying out of Roman towns. The
employment of a common base line for both the town plan and the
centuriated land is documented both in Italy and in other parts of the
empire.[22] The use of *insulae* 75–80 m square, which corresponds to the
usual allotment to a colonist of two *iugera* (0.5 ha approx.), is further
evidence of this relationship. At Pompeii, there was a direct relationship
between parts of the residential districts and the centuriated land to the
north. The street grid of *regio VI* on the northern side of the town was
related directly to the centuriated land outside the city, and several of the
villas in the region were orientated in the same direction as the
centuriated land.[23]

Secondly, at Pompeii, and similarly at Herculaneum, there is little
differentiation within the *insulae* between economic and purely domestic
usage. Recent studies in the distribution of different types of property
within the residential areas are illuminating.[24] Whilst commercial
properties tended naturally to concentrate in those *insulae* which
bordered the busier streets, they are found throughout the city. Even the
large houses, if they had direct access on to the more important streets,
were associated with commercial properties. Conversely, there are only a
few restricted areas where exclusively residential occupation is to be
found. One such area is in the heart of *regio VI* in the north-western
corner of the city, and the lack of commercial properties in the area can
be explained by its relative isolation from major through-routes.

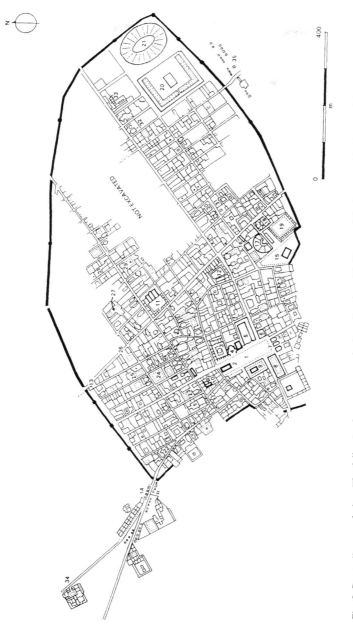

Fig. 8: Pompeii: general plan. The following houses are marked on the plan: 22. House of the Surgeon; 23. House of the Tragic Poet; 24. House of the Faun; 25. House of the Vettii; 26. House of the Golden Cupids; 27. House of the Silver Wedding; 28. House of Lucretius Fronto; 29. House of the Centenary; 30. House of the Cryptoporticus; 31. House of the Menander; 32. House of Loreius Tiburtinus; 33. Villa of Julia Felix; 34. Villa of the Mysteries.

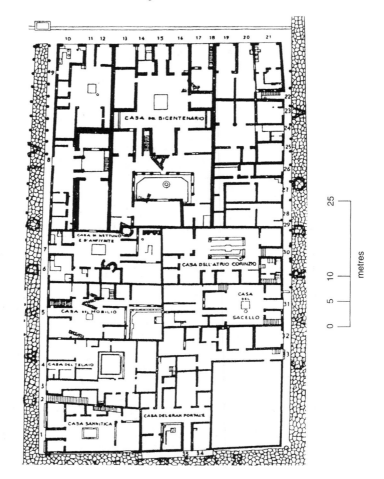

Fig. 9: Herculaneum: plan of *insula V*.

Thirdly, despite the fact that the houses themselves vary in size, shape and internal configuration, there seems to be little social differentiation between areas. A few houses at Pompeii, like the House of the Faun or the House of Pansa in *regio VI*, and the even larger Villa of Julia Felix close to the *palaestra*, occupied complete *insulae*, although in both the House of the Faun and the House of Pansa a row of small one-roomed shops was included in the facade. More usually a variety of houses of differing sizes and shapes occupied the *insulae*, as for example in *insula* V at Herculaneum (fig. 9). Nor is the overall size of the house within an *insula* an indication of the wealth or importance of its owner. Small houses could be richly decorated.

The evidence suggests a complex nexus of relationships within the domestic quarters of Pompeii and Herculaneum. Moreover, the internal arrangement of residential areas was not immutable. Over a period of time residential *insulae* were altered as the ownership of houses changed. These developments had two effects at Pompeii. In the first instance larger houses were subdivided into multiple dwellings, although the social implications of subdividing larger houses remain controversial.[25] Secondly, as in many Graeco-Roman cities of the Mediterranean, space within the walls of Pompeii was finite. Thus, when there was a demand for extra accommodation, houses had to expand vertically. Unfortunately the typical *domus* of Pompeii, which was dominated by the *atrium* (see p. 37 below), meant that often vertical expansion was confined to the addition of small irregular upper rooms.[26] The addition of upper storeys to houses also affected the overall dimensions of the *insulae*, when overhanging balconies and upper rooms, supported by columns, encroached on to the public streets and pavements.

Such encroachment was not confined to Pompeii. Laws in the *Theodosian Code* forbade overhanging balconies, not only because of the increased risk of fire, but also because they provided convenient hideouts from which muggers might attack passing pedestrians.[27] Such additions were not altogether unwelcome to the pedestrian, providing, like the high buildings of Rome before Nero's rebuilding of the city, shade and protection from the elements.[28] In Romanised native towns of Africa, such as Sabratha, external porticoes along the streets, providing shade and protection, were a regular feature of the residential *insulae*.

Pompeii and Herculaneum were essentially residential country towns. Ostia, on the other hand, founded originally as one of a pair of colonies to protect the mouth of the River Tiber, developed into a bustling and populous harbour town. As we have already seen (p. 3), at Rome multiple-occupancy dwellings, termed by Cicero '*insulae*',[29] had long been a feature of residential quarters, and were increasingly to be found elsewhere. Multiple dwellings evolved in response to a rapidly increasing population and the need to provide reasonably priced accommodation in cities, where ground rents were high.

Similarly at Ostia, the rapid development of the port under the emperors Claudius and in particular Trajan and Hadrian, produced the same demand for reasonable accommodation of the sort already to be found at Rome. Purpose-built tenement blocks became the characteristic feature of Ostia, and supplanted the *domus*-type house as the major form of domestic building. They were well built and well planned, belying, to a certain extent, the vivid literary descriptions of the squalor and the dangers to which the inhabitants of such buildings were subject.[30] The Ostian *insulae* were regular and the buildings themselves were often spacious and well lit, with separate access to the upper floors via external staircases.[31]

Ostia itself developed piecemeal (fig. 10). New districts were added as the town expanded, but the alignments of the areas and the roads do not correspond to an overall plan. Figure 11 gives a view of the area around the forum as it was developed under the emperor Hadrian. The district is in general regular, although the regularity is by no means rigidly imposed. Thus, the two main roads which run through the area deviate to pass through the Marina gate and the Laurentine gate respectively. Minor streets then divided the district into building blocks, although the blocks themselves varied in size and shape. Public buildings, barracks, temples, *domus*-style houses and apartment blocks were contiguous and competed for space. As in other towns, the separation of domestic buildings from commercial and industrial establishments was not a feature of the domestic quarters of Ostia. Shops and other commercial premises lined the streets, and behind them stood private houses and apartments (pl. 4). As at Pompeii, even the more prestigious buildings were often fronted by shops.[32] Furthermore, there was little social differentiation in the occupation of such multiple dwellings. Spacious apartments are to be found in the same tenement block as meaner rooms and flats.

Although the tenement blocks of Ostia and Rome were well built, a large population, accommodated in such cramped conditions, brought problems. In general, fire was a constant hazard in the towns and cities of the Empire, and indeed was not confined to Rome. One of Pliny's letters tells of a disastrous fire which destroyed a large part of Nicomedia in Bithynia, and of the steps which he wanted to take in order to prevent a similar occurrence.[33] At the other end of the Roman world Verulamium suffered several destructive fires in the course of its history.[34] Excessively tall buildings were another potential hazard, and at Rome Augustus, Nero and Trajan limited the height of tall buildings.[35] Although there is evidence of inferior construction, with potentially dangerous results if they collapsed, height limits were

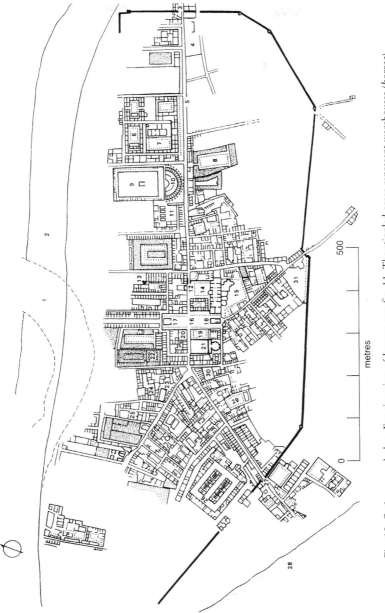

Fig. 10: Ostia: general plan. For situation of houses, see fig. 11. The stippled areas represent warehouses (*horrea*).

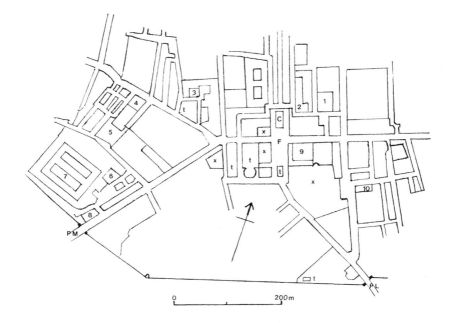

Fig. 11: Ostia: sketch plan of the central area around the Forum. F=Forum; C=Capitolium;
x=public buildings; t=temples; PM=Porta Marina; PL=Porta Laurentina. The
following *insulae*/houses are marked: 1. House of Diana: 2. L-shaped block;
3. House of Amor and Psyche; 4. House of Serapis; 5. House of the Charioteers;
6. House of the Muses; 7. Garden Houses; 8. House of the Nymphaeum; 9. House
of the Triclinia; 10. House of Fortuna Annonaria.

probably imposed for fire prevention. Increasing the population of the
tenement buildings not only increased the risk of fire, but also the height
of the buildings might assist the spread of fire as the flames leapt from
one building to another.

Although the nature of towns and cities was conditioned by their
buildings, it is often forgotten that open space was an important and
integral part of the ancient architecture and the urban landscape (cf.
Chapter 5). Courtyards, either as simple open areas, or surrounded by
colonnades or arcades, were the essential feature of many urban
buildings. In public buildings a colonnaded open space formed the
central feature of *fora*, markets and other commercial buildings,
mansiones, storehouses, *palaestrae* and gymnasia. In addition it was not
unusual to find peristyle courtyards appended to other public buildings.

Thus an important factor, which conditioned the configuration of residential blocks, was the availability and use of free space. As with public buildings, so in a domestic context, courtyards were a ubiquitous feature of houses throughout the Graeco-Roman world and are found from the Greek east to Britain. Nor was the courtyard confined to *domus*-type houses; tenement buildings could also be built around an arcaded courtyard (for example the Tenement of the Muses at Ostia).

Free space, therefore, in an urban context was a valued commodity. The spaciousness of an underdeveloped town such as Silchester, with its gardens, orchards and other forms of cultivated land amid free-standing houses and other buildings, has already been mentioned. In more populous cities, like Pompeii with its high density of occupation, undeveloped space for private use was a particularly prized asset. Gardens were particularly favoured.

Gardens, often ornately decorated with peristyles, sculptures and fountains, and containing flowers, trees and bushes, became the central feature of many houses. A particularly sumptuous example is the garden of the House of Marcus Loreius Tiburtinus. Another is the large tract of land adjoining the rear of the Villa of Julia Felix, close to the *palaestra*, which was planted as an orchard and a vegetable plot, and also contained a fish pond.[36] Not only did the gardens allow air and light into the surrounding rooms, but they also provided open space and gave a sense of the countryside within the city. One is reminded here of the Elder Pliny's comment on the appearance of gardens at Athens. He states that, under the guise of gardens, people possessed luxurious farms and country houses within the city, a practice first introduced by Epicurus.[37] The large houses of late Republican and Imperial Rome were similarly embellished with sumptuous gardens.[38] At Pompeii gardens were not confined to the richer dwellings. Sometimes even those who lived in shops might have access to a small plot of undeveloped land, which they cultivated, at the rear of the establishments.[39] As the urban population expanded, the provision of basic amenities became essential. Water had to be provided for a whole range of domestic, industrial and public purposes. Water distribution to residential areas of a town varied greatly. In some towns there was no provision, and householders had to rely on private wells and cisterns, or had to carry water from the nearest public fountain. At Pompeii water was piped to a number of water towers (*castella*), whence it was distributed to small roadside fountain houses, which were strategically placed at the junctions of streets (pl. 5).

In towns like Ostia and Rome with their large numbers of tenement buildings, the problems of conveniently supplying water to the inhabitants were particularly acute. A system of distribution similar to that at Pompeii, with conveniently placed public street fountains, operated at Ostia and Rome, which, according to Frontinus, had 247 water distribution towers.[40] In some cities, if the supply was sufficient, water was piped directly to individual householders, who paid a fee to the emperor for the service.[41] This happened in Rome, and the archaeological evidence from Ostia, where pipes have been found inscribed with the users' names, and Pompeii confirms that water was introduced into private dwellings (pl. 6). Indeed, a constant threat to the water supply of Rome and, presumably, other cities was the illegal tapping of the public supply by individuals.[42] However, even when public supplies were provided, private wells and cisterns were often maintained and used, as the evidence from the siege of Naples by Belisarius, Justinian's general, proves. When he besieged the city in A.D. 536 he cut the aqueduct. However, this had little effect on the success of the siege because the inhabitants were well supplied with water from wells.[43] Despite the number of aqueducts supplying the city of Rome, wells were still in use in the sixth century A.D.[44] Local civic laws at Pergamon required householders to maintain their private cisterns, even though the city was supplied with water by several aqueducts.[45]

Urban dwelling brought problems of drainage, sewage and sanitation. As the number of buildings increased, so the control of rainwater to avoid damage to property became more urgent. Similarly, an increasing population required adequate sanitary arrangements. The provision of drains and sewers varied according to the level of urbanisation attained by a town and the availability of financial resources. Few towns in Britain had any form of drainage system, and none approached the sophistication of the drainage system of Lindum (Lincoln). In contrast, many of the towns of Italy and the provinces boasted comprehensive drainage systems. Early on a system of drains and sewers was a feature of Rome.[46] The primary purpose of these drainage systems was to control and remove rainwater in order to protect property. Sanitation facilities, on the other hand, often remained rudimentary. Many of the houses at Pompeii were provided with cesspit/latrines, although few, if any, were linked to the street drains.[47] The difficulties of controlling rainwater and removing waste were even more acute in tenement blocks. At Ostia, although communal latrines were to be found on the ground floors of tenements, there is only one recorded example of an upper-storey latrine.[48] The lack of facilities on the upper storeys adds credibility to one of the dangers, mentioned by Juvenal, which pedestrians faced on the streets of Rome when they passed under open upper-storey windows.[49] Public facilities were probably more abundant. Besides the three public latrines and the latrines attached to the bath houses, in addition, throughout the residential areas of Ostia, there were urinals in the form of large earthen jars, which were sunk into the street surface, or were located in the passageways of buildings or shops. The building inscription from Pergamon indicates that cesspits or latrines were to be found throughout the domestic quarters. The householders, grouped into associations, were responsible for organising the removal of the waste.[50]

In fact, much of the responsibility of the maintenance and upkeep of the domestic areas of the cities fell directly on the property owners, with the state acting only in a supervisory role, ensuring that the work was carried out. Thus, the municipal law of Julius Caesar compelled the householders whose properties fronted the streets to maintain the road surfaces and keep them in good repair.[51] In reality, however, it seems unlikely that the well-made streets of cities such as Ostia, Pompeii and elsewhere throughout the Empire could have been adequately maintained by such a system of private responsibility; and so there must have been some way in which the individual commuted his responsibility to the state, presumably for money.

The towns and cities of the Roman world are rightly famous for their public buildings. Often they are the most visible remaining evidence of ancient urban life. Nevertheless, the domestic quarters were an integral part of the Roman city. They were fully integrated into the town, and their arrangement and development reveals a complex nexus of relationships with all other aspects of urban life, economic, social and even political. The houses themselves vary in type, size, complexity and construction; and the analysis of them is the object of study in the succeeding chapters.

NOTES

1. Livy 5.55.2–5; see also Livy 5.42.1–3; 6.4.6; Diodorus Siculus 14.116.8–9.

2. See e.g. Livy 26.27.2.

3. Suetonius, *Nero* 38.2.

30 E. J. OWENS

4. Tacitus, *Annals* 15.38–41. Party walls could be thin. When dying, Metellus Celer, the husband of the infamous Clodia, could knock on the dividing wall between his house and his neighbour's, Q. Catulus, and call him; see Cicero, *pro Caelio* 59.

5. Cicero, *de lege agraria* 2.96.

6. SIG.[3] 141.

7. I would like to thank Mr. B. Bishop, who has made a detailed study of the town plan of Verona, for this information.

8. See G.C. Boon, *Silchester: the Roman Town of Calleva*, 2nd edition (London 1974), 94–95.

9. See *Theodosian Code* 15.1.9 which allowed inhabitants who built private rooms above publicly owned shops and offices to have possession of the property; *Theodosian Code* 15.1.46 prescribed that those who built private houses in the vicinity of public buildings should leave a minimum gap of 15 feet.

10. Suetonius, *Nero* 37.1.

11. See G.A. Mansuelli, 'Marzabotto: dix années de fouilles et de recherches,' *Mélanges d'Archéologie et d'Histoire de l'Ecole française de Rome* 84 (1972), 124–27. Plan in *Roman Public Buildings*, fig. 2.

12. E.g. see Boon, *Silchester*, 158–59.

13. In Apuleius' *Metamorphoses* (2.2.4) Byrrhaena, an aristocratic woman of Hypata, is immediately recognisable as such to the narrator Lucius.

14. See A. Wallace-Hadrill, 'The social structure of the Roman house', *Papers of the British School at Rome* (new series) 43 (1988), 45.

15. Suetonius, *Diuus Iulius* 46.1.

16. See Cicero, *de haruspicum responso* 49; Velleius Paterculus 2.77.1; Suetonius, *Tiberius* 15.1.

17. Plutarch, *Gaius Gracchus* 12.1.

18. Plutarch, *Marius* 32.1.

19. Cicero, *de domo sua* 100; Livius Drusus the younger similarly wanted his house to be visible to all, Velleius Paterculus 2.14.3; see Wallace-Hadrill, 'The social structure of the Roman house', 46.

20. See R.S. Young, 'An industrial district of ancient Athens', *Hesperia* 20 (1951), 272–77.

21. See J. Wacher, *The Towns of Roman Britain* (London 1975), 386.

22. E.g. at Faventia, the plan of which shares a common base line in the Via Aemilia with the surrounding centuriated land.

23. P. Arthur, 'The urbanisation of Pompeii: excavations 1980–1981', *Antiquaries Journal* 66 (1986), 41.

24. See A. Wallace-Hadrill, 'Elites and trade in the Roman town', in A. Wallace-Hadrill and J. Rich (eds), *City and the Country in the Ancient World* (London 1991), 241–72, esp. 260–61.

25. See the recent discussion in ibid., 254–58.

26. See R. Meiggs, *Roman Ostia*, 2nd edition (Oxford 1973), 235.

27. See *Theodosian Code* 15.1.39.

28. Tacitus, *Annals* 15.43.

29. Cicero, *pro Caelio* 17. See the discussion in the Introduction, p. 3.

30. Whilst there were undoubted dangers in high multiple dwellings, the evidence of passages such as Juvenal 3.193–96 and Strabo 5.3.7 (235) has to be put into the context of the Ostian, and indeed the Roman, evidence for multiple dwellings, and the observations of architects such as Vitruvius (e.g. 2.8.17).

31. Obviously there were exceptions to this general picture, see Meiggs, *Roman Ostia*, 250–51.

32. See ibid., 142.

33. Pliny, *Letters* 10. 33.

34. See Wacher, *The Towns of Roman Britain*, 202–25.

35. Augustus: Strabo 5.3.7 (235) (70 feet). Nero: Tacitus, *Annals* 15.43.1 ('cohibita aedificiorum altitudine'). Trajan: *Epitome de Caesaribus* 13.13 (60 feet).

36. See M. Grant, *Cities of Vesuvius: Pompeii and Herculaneum* (Harmondsworth 1976), 123.

37. Pliny, *Natural History* 19.51.

38. See A.G. McKay, *Houses, Villas and Palaces in the Roman World* (London 1975), 128–31. Suetonius, *Nero* 31.1, describes the particularly sumptuous gardens and grounds of Nero's Domus Aurea (for which see Chapter 4, p. 97).

39. Grant, *Cities of Vesuvius*, 125. For a full treatment of gardens, see Chapter 5.

40. Frontinus, *Aqueducts* 2.78.

41. Id. 2.88.

42. One of the problems which hampered the efforts to control the great fire of A.D. 64 at Rome was the diminution of the water supply through illegal tapping; see Tacitus, *Annals* 15.43. See Frontinus, *Aqueducts* 2.75.

43. See Procopius 5.8.44.

44. Id. 5.19.28.

45. Dittenberger, *OGIS* 483, lines 202–23.

46. See note 1 above; the *cloaca maxima*, which drained the Forum and adjoining areas, was constructed as early as the sixth century B.C., see Pliny, *Natural History* 36.104–6.

47. See A. Scobie, 'Slums, sanitation and mortality in the Roman world', *Klio* 68 (1986), 407–22, esp. 409–13; in contrast the latrines of private houses at Delos were so linked to the street drains, see J. Chamonard, *Exploration archéologique de Delos*, VIII (Paris 1924), 182–90.

48. Scobie, 'Slums, sanitation and mortality', 415.

49. Juvenal 3.268–75.

50. Dittenberger, *OGIS* 483, lines 79–84; see also *Digest* 43.23.1.9 which distinguishes between public and private responsibilities for the upkeep of sewers.

51. See F.F. Abbott and A.C. Johnson, *Municipal Administration in the Roman Empire* (Princeton 1926), no. 24, p. 289, lines 29–33.

2

Urban Housing

A. J. BROTHERS

Without doubt the best evidence, both in quality and in quantity, for housing in Roman towns is to be found at Pompeii and Herculaneum, and it is on that evidence that any account, including this one, must inevitably be principally based—the more so because what the architectural writer Vitruvius has to say about houses[1] largely agrees with what we can see to have been the case in the two Campanian towns.

But it would be a great mistake to suppose that our principal evidence is also our only evidence; there are a number of other sites to be considered. Some of these, such as Paestum in Lucania, further south in Italy, and Vasio Vocontiorum (Vaison-la-Romaine) in Provence, show similar styles of housing, but others do not. The differences to be found at some of these other sites—the towns of Roman Britain, for example—can almost certainly be attributed, in part at least, to differences of climate and topography or, as at Ostia, to the different character of the urban environment. Elsewhere the different nature of the evidence is more simply and obviously due to differences of date. The life of Pompeii and Herculaneum came to an abrupt end in A.D. 79, and there are good grounds for thinking that at that time the two towns were in the early stages of a period of considerable social and economic upheaval (see p. 48 below). Earlier sites, such as Etruscan Marzabotto, and ones where urban life continued long after the first century A.D.—Ostia, again, is an obvious case in point—tell us much about precedents, which the visible buildings of Pompeii and Herculaneum have largely concealed, and about later developments, for which Pompeii and Herculaneum can obviously supply no information.

Nevertheless it is right to discuss the houses of Pompeii and Herculaneum first. Of course, these houses show considerable variation among themselves, just as modern houses do today; and, just as today, this is due partly to the wishes or wealth of the owner, partly to the amount of space or the shape of the ground available, partly to the date of the original construction and how far it was altered afterwards, and so on. Even these considerations are not as straightforward as they may seem. It has already been pointed out (see p. 17 above) that the mere size of a house or the area in which it is located may not necessarily reflect the owner's wealth and status, just as today there are poor people who live in grand houses in once-opulent areas which have seen better days, or rich ones who live in well-appointed flats, mews cottages or terraced houses in the crowded centres of our cities and towns. It is obvious that any account may not apply to all houses, or even to any for all of the time; but it should enable us to understand the main elements of the 'typical' form.

The first point to make is that these houses looked inward not outward, and received their light and air from inside not outside. They consisted of rooms grouped round one or more central rooms or courtyards with, at most, only a few small windows in their outside walls (pl. 7), rather like the houses that can still be seen in some eastern countries, especially Arab ones. This made them quieter and cooler in the bustle of town life, as well as less open to burglary and other dangers of urban civilisation. The houses were also relatively low by today's standards: the earlier ones probably had only one storey, and the later ones rarely, if ever, exceeded two; moreover, such second storeys as existed were restricted to certain parts of the house. In the development of these houses there seem to have been two main phases: firstly the purely 'Italic' form of a single set of rooms round a large open one, and secondly the addition to this of a colonnaded courtyard surrounded by further rooms. This addition came about under Greek influence and was usually made at the rear of the original house; it gradually led to alterations in the use, and sometimes also the structure, of the rooms in the older part. The double origin of the parts of the developed house can be seen in the fact that the rooms in the older part have Latin names like *atrium*, *ala* and *tablinum*, while those in the newer part have Greek ones like *peristylium*, *oecus* and *exedra*. Good examples of houses of the earlier type are the House of the Surgeon at Pompeii (fig. 12) and the Samnite House at Herculaneum, while the developed type can be seen in the House of the Faun (fig. 13) and, at a much later period, the House of the Vettii (fig. 14), both at Pompeii.

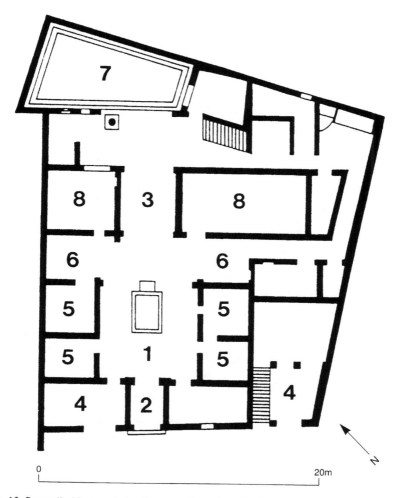

Fig. 12: Pompeii: House of the Surgeon. 1. *atrium*; 2. *fauces*; 3. *tablinum*; 4. shop; 5. bedroom; 6. *ala*; 7. garden; 8. dining room.

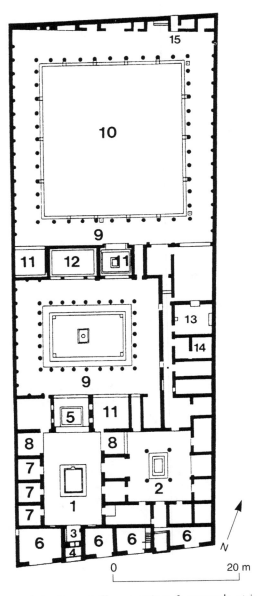

Fig. 13: Pompeii: House of the Faun. 1. Tuscan *atrium;* 2. tetrastyle *atrium;* 3. *fauces;* 4. porch; 5. *tablinum;* 6. shop; 7. bedroom; 8. *ala:* 9. peristyle; 10. garden; 11. dining-room; 12. *exedra;* 13. kitchen; 14. bath; 15. *posticum.*

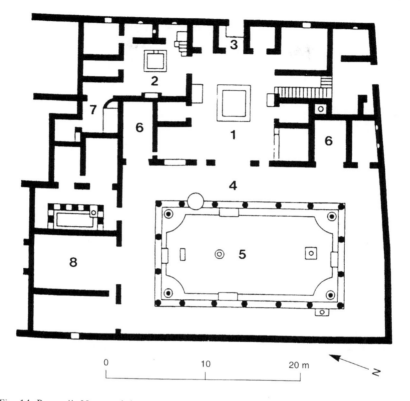

Fig. 14: Pompeii: House of the Vettii. 1. *atrium*; 2. second *atrium*; 3. *fauces*; 4. peristyle;
5. garden; 6. *oecus*; 7. kitchen; 8. dining-room.

The early Italic house is often termed an '*atrium*' house'. This *atrium*
was its principal room, a large and lofty centrally-lit hall which,
according to one theory, had in early times been the main living-room of
the family. There are several suggested derivations of the word *atrium*;
one of the more likely, which supports the 'living-room' theory, is that
the word comes from *ater* (black), because the roof beams would
originally have been blackened by the smoke from the family hearth-fire
which burned in the centre under a small hole in the roof.[2] None of the
houses which we see today preserves this primitive arrangement, but the
feature of the hole in the roof is still there. By later times it had become
a large rectangular opening over the middle of the *atrium*, called a
compluvium, towards which the roof sloped downwards and inwards

from all four sides. In the floor directly under the *compluvium* was a shallow rectangular basin called an *impluvium* into which the rainwater fell.[3] From the *impluvium* there were two outlets. One carried the water to a cistern, which often had a carved ornamental well-head called a *puteal* near the edge of the *impluvium* itself (pl. 8). The other outlet carried off any excess water when the cistern was full, and led under the floor to the street outside. This arrangement reflects earlier practice for the supply of water, and was later supplemented by a piped water-distribution system both at Pompeii and at Herculaneum (see p. 27 above). Some larger *impluvia* contained a fountain (pl. 9) or a statue (as in the case of the dancing faun which gives the House of the Faun its name).

I have already implied that there is more than one theory on the origins of the *atrium*, and no definitive statement about the matter can be made. The theory that it was a living-room, already mentioned, is supported not only by the suggested derivation of *atrium*, but also by the fact that some *atria*, such as those in the House of the Skeleton and the House of the Stags at Herculaneum, have no *impluvium* in them, while excavation has shown that in other houses—the House of the Surgeon is one example—the *impluvium* is a later insertion into what had earlier been a simple floor. Moreover, one of the types of *atrium* listed by Vitruvius (see below) had an overall roof with neither a *compluvium* nor an *impluvium*. The other theory is that the *atrium* was originally a courtyard on to which the roof encroached by gradual extension of the surrounding eaves. This suggestion is supported by evidence from Marzabotto, where some of the excavated houses contain pebbled courtyards on to which rooms open. The absence of *impluvia* in some houses at Pompeii and Herculaneum, whether only early on or at the time the towns were destroyed, can, of course, be invoked to support this theory equally as well as the 'living-room' one. Further evidence is often cited from Etruscan tombs, some of which bear a close resemblance to early *atrium* houses, but it may not be particularly compelling. Even though some, like the famous Tomb of the Volumnii near Perugia (fig. 15), have central *atria* covered by a pitched and beamed roof, the central space of a tomb, whether meant to represent a room or a courtyard, could not have been left open, but would have had to be covered as a precaution against tomb-robbers.

Vitruvius[4] distinguishes five types of *atrium*. The first, assumed, as its name implies, to have been the original one, he calls 'Tuscan', and this is the type most commonly found. Here the roof was carried on a complicated system of beams whose only support was the outer walls of the room. But to leave the beams otherwise unsupported must have been difficult, and other types evolved where they also rested on columns standing round the *impluvium*. This, of course, tended to obscure the view through the *atrium*, but the use of the columns made the area look much more imposing and probably added to the impression of the owner's wealth and status.[5] The 'tetrastyle' *atrium* had four of these columns, one at each corner of the *impluvium*. The 'Corinthian' *atrium* had a larger *impluvium* surrounded by a whole colonnade of columns— in the House of Castor and Pollux at Pompeii there are twelve of them, and in the House of Epidius Rufus, also at Pompeii (pl. 10), there are sixteen. These two types of *atrium*, as their names and the very use of columns imply, show Greek influence and are therefore later.[6] Vitruvius' fourth type is labelled 'displuviate'; it appears to have had a *compluvium*

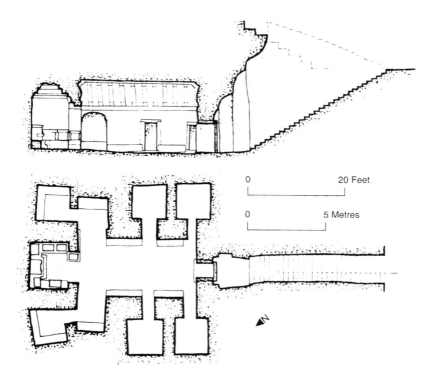

0   20 Feet

0   5 Metres

Fig. 15: Tomb of the Volumnii, near Perugia. Section and plan.

(and therefore presumably an *impluvium* too), but the roof, instead of sloping inwards towards the *compluvium*, sloped outwards away from it, throwing most of the rainwater off. Neither Pompeii nor Herculaneum has so far produced any certain examples of this, but there exists an early model from Clusium (Chiusi) (fig. 16) which shows the type well, and the roofs of some tombs, notably the *tomba di Mercareccia* at Tarquinia,[7] reflected the arrangement. The fifth and last type in the list is the 'testudinate' or 'tortoise' *atrium*; this had no *compluvium* and therefore no *impluvium*, but a complete overall roof, probably in the form of a low pyramid. This may have been the case in the House of the Skeleton and the House of the Stags, mentioned above, though in both of these the roof has now been totally destroyed. Some larger houses had two *atria*; in the House of the Faun (fig. 13) one is Tuscan and the other tetrastyle.

If the *atrium* had indeed been the main living-room of the family in early times, it had certainly ceased to be so in the houses we now see. In these, it seems to have been a fairly formal area, used for specific social functions, some of them quite public like the morning *salutatio* (greeting) of the master of the house by his clients.[8] Like the grand entrance halls of some great English houses, it was probably only sparsely furnished, with perhaps a few couches, cupboards or tables.

Fig. 16: Model of a 'displuviate' *atrium* from Clusium (Chiusi).

Sometimes the strong-box (*arca*) of the master of the house containing the family's valuables stood against one of the walls; the shrine of the household gods (*lararium*) sometimes occupied a similar position, as in the House of the Menander at Pompeii; sometimes the herm (portrait bust) of the master stood against the wall opposite the door, so as to be seen immediately upon entry—it can still be seen there in the House of Caecilius Jucundus in Pompeii and the House of the Bronze Herm at Herculaneum; and sometimes, too, by the *impluvium* stood a table (*cartibulum*) (pl. 9), possibly representing the original family meal-table, where ceremonial bronze vessels for use in household cult were placed.

The *atrium* was reached from the street by a narrow passage called the *fauces* (literally 'throat'). The front door was either right at the front of this, or set a little way back in it, leaving a porch (*vestibulum*) in front. It was in the floor of the *fauces* that the various well-known 'beware of the dog' mosaics were set, and sometimes the word HAVE ('greetings') was set in the pavement just outside. On the outside, too, the doorway itself was often elaborate and imposing, framed by pilasters or semi-columns of stone or stucco-covered brickwork. This was, after all, the way in which the owner presented himself to the outside world, and visitors, of whatever rank, were meant to be impressed. Good examples can be seen at the House of the Faun, the Villa of Julia Felix at Pompeii and the House of the Grand Portal at Herculaneum; there are many others (cf. pl. 7). The actual doors were wooden and usually double. They did not hang from the doorposts by hinges as our doors do today, but swung on pivots which turned in sockets in the threshold and lintel; the metal linings of these sockets can still sometimes be seen in the threshold. The doors were fastened by bolts and sometimes by heavy iron locks as well. At night they could be made more secure by a heavy wooden prop set into a socket in the middle of the *fauces* floor and wedged against the centre of the doors themselves. Occasionally, as in the House of the Bull at Pompeii, there was also a small door in the side wall of the *vestibulum* just in front of the main doors; this gave on to a short passage leading past these, which opened into the *fauces* behind them, thus obviating the necessity of opening the main doors every time a single individual wanted to enter. The elaborate nature of all these arrangements for security clearly demonstrates the dangers which were around in the streets, especially at night.

At the back of the *atrium* in the centre of its rear wall was a large room called a *tablinum* (pl. 8). This opened on to the *atrium* along its whole width, but could be closed off by curtains or a folding partition; a partition of this sort has been wonderfully preserved in the House of the Wooden Partition at Herculaneum. The posts at either side of the entrance to the *tablinum* were often treated as pilasters and joined by a cornice, so forming an architecturally impressive feature of the *atrium* when seen as one entered by the *fauces* opposite. In early times the *tablinum* often opened on to a verandah at the back which looked over the garden; it was possibly the master's sleeping-room. Later, when other bedrooms came into use, the rear entrance was closed. The room now became used for more formal purposes, but often the *lectus genialis* or ceremonial marriage-couch still stood there to recall its former use. Later, if a peristyle court was added behind, the *tablinum* was sometimes again opened out at the back.

The *fauces*, *atrium* and *tablinum*, all on the same axis, formed a very suitable 'theatre' for formal functions such as the *salutatio*, and for the reception of visitors to conduct business with the master of the house— particularly those visitors who did not enjoy the closeness of contact with him which might earn admission to the more intimate ánd secluded parts of his house. In this connection it is important to remember that the Romans who lived in this sort of house rarely had an office or workplace as we do; much of their business was transacted at home. Indeed, as Wallace-Hadrill stresses, 'the Roman house was a constant focus of public life'.[9] As one passed through the doors along the (often richly decorated) *fauces*, the eye was naturally drawn to the *tablinum*, and sometimes out into the garden or peristyle court beyond, while at the end of the *fauces* the width and height of the *atrium*, with its *impluvium* bathed in a shaft of light from above, was striking and impressive. It all helped to create an appropriate atmosphere as the owner showed his public face in his own home.

On either side of the *fauces* at the front of the house were one or more small rooms. Originally these were probably bedrooms or service- or storage-rooms for the house, and sometimes they remained so; but a common feature in Pompeii and Herculaneum is to find that they were later converted into shops (*tabernae*) facing on to the street on either side of the entrance (see p. 22 above and fig. 13). Whether these *tabernae* were still under the control of the owner of the house is not always clear, but the fact that they are often completely shut off, with no access at all from the house itself, would seem to indicate that many were not. This late development is only one of a number of trends (see p. 48 below) which indicate the start of the period of social and economic change already referred to.

On both sides of the *atrium* was a further series of small rooms, most of which seem to have been bedrooms (*cubicula*). In these, the position of the bed was often marked by a change in the mosaic pattern on the floor, by a change in the pattern of the ceiling or by a low raised platform where the bed stood. Sometimes the bed seems almost to be set in its own alcove.

Finally, the *atrium* had two 'wings' or *alae*, rooms—perhaps 'spaces' or 'areas' would be better—on either side of it. Usually they were situated towards the back, on either side of the *tablinum*, but sometimes, as in the House of Epidius Rufus (pl. 10), they were in the middle of each side of the *atrium* itself. They were open to the *atrium* along all their length; but what they were used for is quite uncertain. It is said that in earlier times they contained the images of the family ancestors, or they may have had something to do with the formalities of the *salutatio*. Later they may have been used for dining or even served as wardrobes; perhaps too they served to let in additional light through small external windows. Their function must remain a mystery, perhaps because they were a relic of the fashions and living habits of earlier times.

This, then, was the basic form of the so-called Italic house, sometimes with a garden or small open court at the back, and quite a few houses, both at Pompeii and Herculaneum, remained in that form, with redecoration and comparatively minor alterations from time to time. However, where there was the space available, many others had a whole new section added, reminiscent of the courtyard houses of the Greeks. This was almost always at the rear, where the garden had once been, but there are exceptions, such as the House of the Stags (fig. 17) and the House of the Mosaic Atrium, both at Herculaneum, where, because of the shape of the space available, the 'Greek' part runs at right angles to the *atrium* section. When it was at the back, this new part was usually connected to the old one by a corridor (called, like most of the components in it, by a Greek word, in this case *andron*), which ran from the *atrium* to the right or left of the *tablinum* (pl. 8).

The central feature of this new part was a formal *peristylium* or peristyle court, a small garden enclosed by a colonnade on three or on all four sides; it was around this that the rooms ranged. This garden was planted with trees, shrubs and other plants, and, equally importantly, usually contained a variety of pools, fountains and statuary (see p. 27 above). There are many beautiful examples in both towns, such as that in the House of the Golden Cupids in Pompeii. The most famous

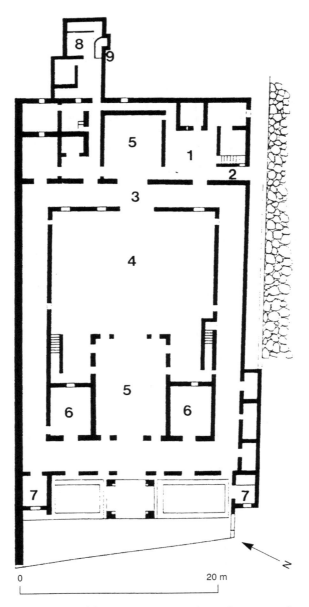

Fig. 17: Herculaneum: House of the Stags. 1. *atrium*; 2. *fauces*; 3. *cryptoporticus*; 4. garden;
5. dining-room; 6. *oecus*; 7. *diaeta*; 8. kitchen; 9. latrine.

example, however, is the one in the House of the Vettii (pl. 11 and fig. 14), though, probably because this is a late house (of the early Empire) and the traditional forms of the older part were by then less in vogue, it has no *tablinum* and its peristyle opens straight from the comparatively small and insignificant *atrium*.[10] It is a sad comment on today's *mores* that most of the beautiful sculptures which it once contained—and such as have not already been stolen—have had to be removed for safe-keeping; the same has happened to the masks and carved marble discs which once hung between the columns in the peristyle of the House of the Golden Cupids.

Behind the colonnades of the peristyle were rooms of various types. Among these, dining-rooms were most popular and are very frequently found. The dinner-party (*cena*) was a great institution, and, although some must have been strictly family affairs, many were for the entertainment of friends, official guests and business associates, where much negotiation, discussion and bargaining must have taken place—the business lunch is nothing new. Here again we have the intermingling of public and private (see p. 42 above and note 9). The old idea that the *atrium* section of a house was *only* for the business side of a householder's life and that the peristyle section was *only* for the family and for purely social intercourse with a very few intimate friends simply does not tally with what we know of the Roman way of life. Though sometimes referred to by the Roman name *cenationes*, these dining-rooms were often known as *triclinia*, a Greek word derived from the traditional three couches on which the diners reclined. The position of these couches was often marked by a change in the mosaic pattern on the floor, with the more elaborate motifs where the diners could see them, rather than under the couches themselves;[11] sometimes, too, low plinths show us where the couches were. In these arrangements, we are reminded of the indications of the position of the beds in the bedrooms. As we can still see from the excavated remains, it was not at all uncommon for a house to have more than one of these dining-rooms. Literature gives us further evidence: Vitruvius[12] discusses the positioning of dining-rooms for winter, for spring and autumn, and for summer, and in Petronius' *Satyricon*, Trimalchio says he has four, and (possibly) one upstairs as well.[13] Sometimes what was obviously a summer dining-room was not in the house at all, but outside in the garden.

Some of the other rooms round the peristyle were undoubtedly further bedrooms. These would have been lighter and airier than those in the older part of the house, and probably cooler in summer as well.

It might follow that the bedrooms which opened on to the *atrium* were latterly more for winter use; certainly they could be more easily heated by braziers. Even bedrooms were not strictly private, but business could be transacted in them, though presumably only when it was of a confidential nature and conducted with true intimates;[14] here again, the incorrectness of the view that the peristyle section of the house was somehow for the family only is reinforced.

Other rooms were the *oecus*, a reception hall perhaps also used for dining, and often one of the most elaborately decorated rooms in the house; the *diaeta*, an airy, open room used for rest and relaxation (almost like a conservatory or summerhouse); and the *exedra*, a broad and sometimes deep recess open to the colonnade along all its width, often situated at the rear of the peristyle and thus corresponding to the *tablinum* of the *atrium* section which it in many ways resembled. Of course, not all houses, especially the smaller ones, had all of these rooms, and in many cases identifying them as such is difficult and disputed—is a particular room an *oecus* or a *diaeta*, for example? Even the classification by type is not certain; Vitruvius discusses *exedrae* and *oeci*, but does not mention *diaetae*.[15] He distinguishes several types of *oecus*: Corinthian, tetrastyle, Egyptian and Cyzicene. A fine example of an Egyptian *oecus*, resembling, as he says, a basilica, is to be found at the back of the *atrium* in the House of the Mosaic Atrium in place of the traditional *tablinum*.

The contrast between the open and light peristyle section of the house and the much more enclosed and dark *atrium* part, illuminated only by the light from the *compluvium* and, at most, a few small windows, can be seen from the reconstructions at Pompeii and Herculaneum to have been great. But we have seen that a family/public distinction between the uses of the two parts does not hold good; and neither an informal/formal nor a summer/winter contrast can be pushed too far. It may be that there were general tendencies towards such distinctions owing to the different physical structure of the two parts. But it would be dangerous to go much further than that, and in later houses with insignificant *atria* even that conservative statement of the case may be misleading.

Into the *atrium*/peristyle complex a number of other essential rooms were inserted, but at various points and with less regular positioning in the overall plan. The most obvious of these are the slaves' quarters, and these were often situated in what was a more general service area. Slaves, of course, moved about the whole house, as secretaries, ladies' maids, nurses for the children, stewards, waiters and so on; even at night, some would be stationed outside the family bedrooms. But they, like other slaves who had less regular contact with the family, had their own quarters where they slept and, presumably, relaxed when 'off duty'—if such a term can ever be used of a Roman slave. These quarters were, as might be expected, small and cramped, and very plain compared to the family's rooms. They are often difficult to identify today, especially if the rest of the house is not particularly grand, and, if they are sometimes not evident at all, that may be because they were not in the service area but in attics and upper storeys which have now disappeared. But in some houses, their location is reasonably clear. In the House of the Faun (fig. 13), for instance, the secondary, tetrastyle *atrium* is obviously the centre of the domestic area, and behind it service- and storage-rooms, with what seem to be slaves' quarters among them, are squeezed in to the east of the spacious peristyle which extends beyond the width of the main Tuscan *atrium* in front of it. An even clearer example can be seen in the House of the Vettii (fig. 14). Here the service area and the slaves' bedrooms are grouped round a separate small courtyard with its own *lararium*, which opens directly off the main *atrium* to the right of the entrance; it would seem that the notorious and explicit small paintings of sexual intercourse which adorn some of the walls were meant for the eyes of the slaves and not the family!

In both of these houses the kitchen is, quite naturally, prominent in the service area. This was almost always surprisingly small, considering the scale of the entertaining that went on. In it the hearth, an oblong structure built of masonry, was the dominant feature (pl. 12); the fire burned on the top of it, and often there was a hollow underneath it for storing fuel and keeping it dry. On and around it stood the cooking pots, and above it there was often a small window to carry off the smoke and sometimes, probably, a hole in the roof as well. Sometimes, too, we find that the kitchen contained a small oven for baking, but with the frequency of mills, bakeries and bakers' shops in Pompeii (and, presumably, Herculaneum too), it is not surprising that many households managed adequately without one.

The latrine was another feature of this area of the house; it too was small, and it was often near the kitchen, as in the House of the Stags where it is right next door. This is surprising to our way of thinking when we are so concerned with hygiene, but for the Romans the availability of water in that part of the house—particularly where it came 'on tap' from the town's piped supply—may have been a more important consideration. Often near the kitchen, too, and for the same reason, was the bath suite if there was one. It is quite natural that only larger houses had this as a rule, since both towns were well supplied with public baths—three have so far been unearthed in Pompeii and two in Herculaneum. Good examples can be seen in the House of the Faun and the House of the Menander, and also in the House of the Dolphin, an *atrium*/peristyle house in Vasio;[16] there are numerous others. Often the suite was only large enough for one or two people at a time and contained only a *caldarium* (hot room) and *tepidarium* (warm room), but some were larger and included a *frigidarium* (cold room) and *apodyterium* (changing room) as well; the heating arrangements were the same as for the public baths, though on a much reduced scale. Incidentally, the siting of both latrine and baths in the service area of the house shows that this was not an area which the family and its guests did not normally enter, and underlines that intermingling of slave and free in the house which has already been referred to.

Some larger houses, the House of the Faun and the House of the Menander again being examples, had a stable which opened on to a street or alley at the back or side, and/or a rear entrance called a *posticum*. Finally, most houses contained a number of rooms for storage, as might be expected.

As the life of Pompeii and Herculaneum approached its end, various changes were taking place in the form of these houses. One of them, the downgrading, as it were, of the *atrium* in the design of some houses of the early Empire, often accompanied by the absence of the *tablinum* (see p. 45 above), may have been due to changes in fashion, taste or the pattern of family and social life. But most of the others are the result of external pressures of an economic nature. The sprawling *atrium*/peristyle house was extremely wasteful of space, and, as land values rose, the population increased and a merchant class arose to challenge the dominance of the local aristocracy more and more, the old style of house could not remain unaltered. The separation from the house of rooms at the front on either side of the *fauces* and their conversion into shops has already been referred to. Sometimes the changes of this sort were more drastic and sweeping. In the House of Pansa at Pompeii, for instance, considerable areas round the house—small separate dwellings, a bakery and shops—were rented out, and a notice advertising the renting of some of them still survives; one shop and one of the dwellings are still in fact connected to the house, and it seems reasonable to suppose that at least some of the others had once also been integral parts of it.

If there was no more room to extend the house outwards or there were economic incentives not to do so, the obvious alternative was to extend upwards (see p. 23 above). Thus we find that the number of second storeys tends to increase at this time. The natural place for this to happen was at the front of the house over the rooms round the *atrium*, and indeed the very height of the *atrium* itself may have facilitated this. These extra rooms were reached by internal stairs, but what they were used for is by no means always clear, simply because they have survived far less well than the rooms underneath them; some at least seem to have been dining-rooms or bedrooms. Sometimes they projected over the pavement at the front, supported on beams, as in the House of the Balcony at Pompeii and the Samnite House and the House of the Wooden Partition (pl. 7) at Herculaneum; in the Samnite House these upper rooms over the main entrance were divided off and reached by a separate steep stairway from the street. It is in the Samnite House that the most complete and beautiful example of a full two-storied *atrium* can be seen; elegant Ionic columns, joined by a balustrade pierced by lozenge-shaped small openings, run all round at first floor level, and at the back of the *atrium*, where there are no rooms behind them, this surround is completely open and lets in the light and air, making this *atrium* far different from many, more gloomy others.

Although the *atrium*/peristyle house was the principal type of housing in both Pompeii and Herculaneum, it was not the only one; there are plenty of examples of humbler dwellings. All three sets of public baths at Pompeii, for example, occupy only the centre of the blocks in which they are built, and are flanked on two sides by rows of shops facing outwards on to the street; the shops follow a more or less regular pattern and have first-floor living accommodation above them, reached by flights of stairs either inside the shops themselves or leading up from the street. Many other shops, bars, small workshops and so on must have exhibited a similar arrangement, with the owner, manager or tenant and his family living in comparatively modest style above his place of work. Equally humble living quarters can be seen in the Trellis House at Herculaneum (pl. 13). This is poorly built, with a frame of brick and wood filled with cane trellis-work and rubble and stuccoed over. This material is known as *opus craticium*, and Vitruvius wishes it had never been invented because, despite its cheapness and speed of erection, it is very prone to the dangers of fire and collapse.[17] Upper storeys or party walls built in this way are quite common, but this house is the only known example of its use for a whole building. It consists of two apartments, one reached down a dark entrance-passage and the other by a separate stairway from the street. The small rooms are ranged round a tiny courtyard with a well; at the front there is a shop with a workroom behind it on the ground floor, while on the first floor a verandah and a small room project over the full width of the pavement, supported by brick columns.

But perhaps the most interesting example of poorer housing is the large block situated on the western side of *Insula Orientalis II* at Herculaneum. The front of this block opens on to *Cardo V* and it backs on to the *palaestra* at the eastern limit of the present excavations; it is almost 100 m long and still rises to some 10 or 12 m in height, probably having been considerably higher in antiquity. Except for the imposing entrance to the *palaestra* towards its southern end, the whole of the frontage is taken up by a number of shops and workshops, a dye-house, a bakery and a mill. Most of these have rear premises connected with the businesses rather than for residential use, and most have internal stairs leading to living accommodation either on an upper floor or, more often, on a mezzanine immediately above the commercial premises. But there are two flights of stairs, one about halfway along and the other at the northern end, which lead directly from the street to the upper floors. Their existence, coupled with the presence of the mezzanine accommodation in most shops and strengthened by some evidence for landings on the first floor of the block, points strongly to the fact that most of the building above the ground floor was occupied by apartments which were quite independent of the commercial properties below them. We have no way now of knowing very much about what these apartments were like, but the whole arrangement of the block is in many ways reminiscent of the great apartment blocks in other Roman towns, particularly Ostia, to which we must now turn our attention.

It is quite clear that apartment blocks (*insulae*)[18] existed in Rome itself earlier than at Herculaneum or at Ostia, which is the town where the best surviving remains of such buildings are now to be found.[19] In the capital buildings of several storeys are recorded as early as the late third century B.C.—at any rate if Livy is to be believed when he includes among the portents of 218 B.C. an incident where an ox climbed to the third storey of a house in the *Forum Boarium*.[20] By the reign of Augustus, the evidence is much surer: Augustus himself set a height limit of 70 Roman feet (20.7 m) for buildings adjoining the public streets,[21] and Vitruvius, referring to the majesty of Rome and the unlimited number of her citizens, says that circumstances forced the Romans to have recourse to high buildings and mentions 'several' and 'various' storeys.[22] Physical remains of *insulae* at Rome are few, but one example exists, largely unnoticed by today's tourists, at the very heart of the ancient city. It stands close by the foot of the long flight of steps leading up to the Church of S. Maria in Ara Coeli, which is on the site of the Temple of Juno Moneta on the ancient citadel (*arx*), and it is built against the rock of the Capitol hill itself. The present remains are of four storeys, the first with a mezzanine floor, and appear to be the rear section of a four-sided construction built round a colonnaded courtyard. Only the top two storeys are easily visible above the level of the modern pavement.[23] In addition, the *Forma Urbis* provides evidence for some ground plans of *insulae* (fig. 1), though, of course, it can tell us nothing about their height. We can be reasonably certain, however, that the erection of such buildings in the capital was given even greater impetus by the reconstruction after the fire of Rome in A.D. 64 (cf. p. 8). These new Roman *insulae* must have employed the latest materials and techniques, with the result that when, some forty or fifty years later, they began to be built at Ostia too, their form had been perfected, and the inhabitants there could look to Roman architects and builders for inspiration and practical help.

There is little doubt that until well into the first century A.D. the urban housing of Ostia was very similar to that of Pompeii and Herculaneum. Even though later rebuilding has destroyed much of the evidence, it appears that *atrium*/peristyle houses—not always only for the well-to-do—were the norm, predominating among the same sort of cramped accommodation above shops and similar premises which we have noted in the two Campanian towns. It is not difficult to identify the conditions which gave rise to the need for sudden and drastic changes to this pattern. By the beginning of our era at the latest, the lower reaches of the Tiber had become totally inadequate to function as Rome's port. When, in response to this, Claudius built a new harbour some 4 km north of the river mouth and connected it by a canal to the river itself, greater prosperity and a growth of population in the town must have been a fairly immediate result. But Claudius' harbour achieved only limited success, and it was the building of a second, safer and inner harbour by Trajan which must have brought an even greater prosperity, and an even greater need for more housing. From this period until the time of Marcus Aurelius (reigned A.D. 161–180), great changes took place, in which the building of more traditional houses seems to have been almost completely abandoned in favour of the erection of *insulae*.

These apartment blocks exhibit considerable variety among themselves, and in an account such as this it is no more possible to cover all
examples than it is with houses. But, as in the latter case, trends and
patterns can be picked out to give a general picture of the type as a whole.

The first point that strikes one is, of course, their presumed height,
though the difficulties presented in being precise about this are obvious.
Only occasionally, as in the case of the House of Diana (pl. 14 and fig.
18), do we have definitive evidence of more than two storeys in the
surviving ruins, and the thickness of the walls in this and in other
examples where even less has survived is not necessarily a good guide to
height, since Roman walls were often built thicker than was strictly
necessary.[24] But some indication of an upper limit can be given by the
fact that Trajan had reduced the building height at Rome to 60 Roman
feet (17.75 m) (cf. p. 24 and n. 35), and that the height of Ostia's
principal temple (*Capitolium*)—some 21 m or 70 Roman feet, set as it is
on an extraordinarily high podium—must have been planned so as to
dominate the crowded buildings which surrounded it (fig. 11). As to the
number of storeys which the *insulae* contained, upper storeys, occupied
perhaps by the poorer classes, may well have been less high than those
beneath them, so calculation by straight division of storeys into probable
height may be misleading. We can only say that four or even five storeys
are perfectly possible, but we cannot be sure.

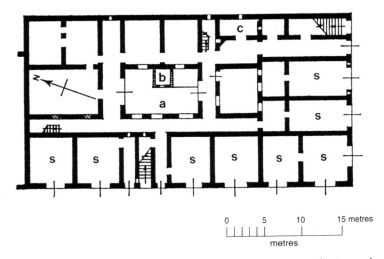

Fig. 18: Ostia: House of Diana, ground floor. *a.* courtyard; *b.* cistern; *c.* latrine; *s.* shop.

A factor which undoubtedly contributed to the success of the new apartment blocks was the perfection of the use of brick-faced concrete, coupled with the efficient organisation of the brick industry; consequently their facades were treated quite differently from those of Pompeian houses. The brick facing was not stuccoed over, but treated as a feature in itself, where relieving arches, the surrounds of doors and windows, and pilasters or semi-columns flanking doorways, provided variety and added character—an effect sometimes heightened by the use of paint to highlight some of these details. Another feature of the facades which contrasts greatly with those of *atrium*/peristyle houses is the frequency of sizeable windows and doors, whose regular or otherwise deliberate arrangement added interest to the design. The doorways not only led into the ground floor or gave on to staircases leading to the upper floors, but were often those of independent shops ranged round the outside of the block, now placed there as an integral part of the initial design and not, as so often at Pompeii and Herculaneum, as a result of subsequent alteration. These shops often had small windows above their doorways, which illuminated the shopkeepers' accommodation inside on a mezzanine floor. The main windows were often fairly large and were, of course, a necessity in apartment blocks; their arrangement was naturally dictated by the location and size of the rooms they lit, but aesthetic considerations also played a part. Aesthetics must also have been responsible for the external balconies which are a feature of many facades, because many of them seem to have been too shallow to be practical and, more obviously, some are not aligned with the levels of the floors inside. The balconies were carried on beams or corbels, or sometimes even on fairly sophisticated brick vaulting. This last feature, together with many of the others just mentioned, can clearly be seen in the House of Diana (pl. 14), a building dating from the middle of the second century A.D.

Sometimes the external windows, however many and however large, were not enough, most obviously where, as in the case of the House of Diana and the House of the Triclinia,[25] one or more of their sides abutted directly on to other buildings. The solution in these instances was to build round a central courtyard, so that rooms which could obtain no light from outside at least got it from inside. The courtyard was sometimes surrounded by a colonnade, as in the House of the Muses, the House of Serapis and the House of the Charioteers, and this occasionally rises above the ground floor. The House of Diana illustrates another convenience which could be afforded by a central court, for it contains a cistern as a communal source of water; in other *insulae* the numerous tenants simply had to rely on the public supply. Latrines seem to have been comparatively few, usually no more than one on each floor, if that; the fairly large one just inside one of the entrances in the House of Diana may have been used by all the inhabitants of the building.

Other arrangements of what we would call high-density housing were, of course, possible. One is what are usually termed the 'Garden Houses' (fig. 19), where two identical blocks, each divided by a corridor into two symmetrical halves, are set back to back in the centre of a large garden provided with no fewer than six fountains. Another is L-shaped, with the two limbs backing on to a garden (fig. 20); the long arm consists of two identical blocks, without any shops, set side by side, the House of the Infant Bacchus and the House of the Paintings, while the short arm contains the larger and deeper House of Jupiter and Ganymede, this time with shops included, and with its own court opening on to the garden. In both these examples, and particularly in the case of the 'Garden Houses', the provision of gardens when building land must have been at a premium implies strongly that the tenants would have been fairly wealthy people who were willing to pay for the extra amenity.

There are other indications, too, that apartments in *insulae* were by no means always for the poor. As in Rome, where the upper classes were using them by the first century B.C.,[26] so in Ostia many of them were obviously not mean or cheap, and in this they belie the impression given in the well-known descriptions by such writers as Juvenal and Martial (see p. 24 above). Not only were the *insulae* themselves almost always well designed and stoutly built, but some apartments were clearly large and well decorated. It is not easy now, of course, to distinguish with total accuracy where one apartment ends and another begins, but some seem to have extended over two floors, or at least to have contained a mezzanine floor as an integral part of them. As with rented accommodation today, that of Ostia must have ranged from the spacious and fairly luxurious apartment to one or two rooms rented—not necessarily on a permanent basis—by poor families or individuals. If Juvenal and Martial concentrated on the latter type, it is because it suited the purpose of their satire to paint an unpleasant picture of danger and discomfort, and Juvenal, at least, had his own axe to grind. And if we see a good number of well-appointed flats and maisonettes, that will be because blocks may well have contained a mixture of accommodation of varying standard, and in those cases the poorer sort will have tended to be on the upper floors which have now disappeared.

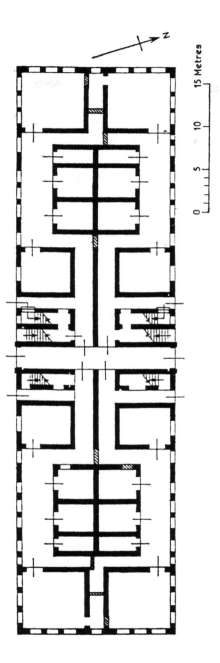

Fig. 19: Ostia: Garden Houses, one of the two central blocks, ground floor.

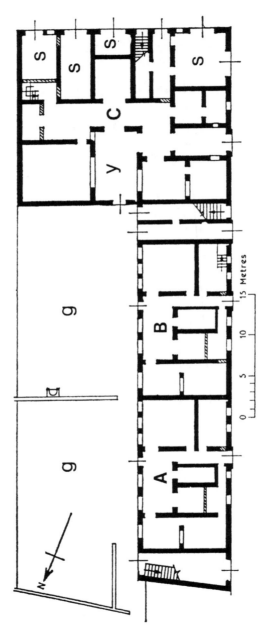

Fig. 20: Ostia: L-shaped block, ground floor. A. House of the Infant Bacchus; B. House of the Paintings; C. House of Jupiter and Ganymede. g: garden; y: courtyard; s. shop.

Just as Ostia provides us with the best evidence for the change from the *domus* to the *insula*, it also bears very clear testimony to a further change back to the *domus* in the later Empire. As with the first of these changes, the second one, too, was the result primarily of economic factors. From the late second century A.D. onwards, the prosperity of the town, together with that of others throughout the Empire, began to decline, and it is natural that this decline should have led to a decrease in population and a resulting excess of accommodation, particularly perhaps that for rent. Excess of accommodation quickly leads to a fall in rents, and it can easily be imagined that the owners of Ostia's apartment blocks could no longer afford to look after them properly or, more fundamentally, did not bother to rebuild them if they were destroyed in one of the frequent fires which were such a feature of urban life in the Roman world. There was thus more room available for those who still wanted to live in the town, and in the third and fourth centuries A.D. the *domus* came back into its own.

But these new houses were very different from the old *atrium/* peristyle ones. They are sometimes called 'peristyle houses' because the rooms faced on to a central area, often containing a pool or fountain, and this area, sometimes paved, sometimes laid out as a garden, was usually flanked on one, two or three sides by a colonnade or portico. But it is not really possible to go much beyond this very general description of them, since their layout varied considerably. One important factor contributing to this variety was the fact that many of them were designed so as to incorporate the walls of earlier buildings, particularly those of ruined or demolished *insulae*; under these circumstances even such limited uniformity as we have seen with the earlier houses and with *insulae* could scarcely be achieved.

However, the houses do exhibit some recurring features, though they may not all occur together in any one example. One of these is the presence of one room which is markedly larger than the others, often at the far side of the court or garden from the entrance (compare the position of the *tablinum* opposite the *fauces* in the *atrium* house); it seems natural to suppose that this was the main living-room. Other features include the existence of an under-floor heating system in some of the rooms (not something that is found in *insulae*), the presence of a *nymphaeum*, a liking for marble as flooring and as wall decoration, and 'a marked taste for apses and for triple-arched columnar screens of a type widely used in late antiquity'[27]—this last often giving a decidedly Byzantine feel to the building. All these features can be seen well in the

small House of Cupid and Psyche (fig. 21), built around A.D. 300; other
good examples are the House of the Nymphaeum and the House of
Fortuna Annonaria. In the House of Cupid and Psyche a long but fairly
narrow area—probably a roofed hall rather than an open court—is
flanked on the left by four rooms, and on the right, after a room leading
to a small latrine, by a screen of columns, once joined by arches, which
opens on to a garden. At the far side of the garden is a large *nymphaeum*;
this has five marble-clad semicircular recesses, above and behind which
are five corresponding niches, alternately semicircular and rectangular,
the piers between them fronted by free-standing columns supporting
brick arches. It is noteworthy that this garden and *nymphaeum* occupy
about one-third of the ground-floor area of the building. At the end of

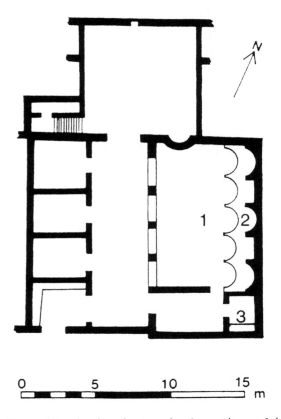

Fig. 21: Ostia: House of Cupid and Psyche. 1. garden; 2. *nymphaeum*; 3. latrine.

the hall the dominant large room is, as so often, entered up two steps which raise it above the level of the rest of the ground floor; it has a particularly elaborate and beautiful floor of coloured marbles in *opus sectile* and remains of marble panels on its walls, as has one of the four smaller rooms already mentioned.

Naturally, the picture given by the urban housing of Italy, varied though it is, does not hold good for the whole of the Roman Empire. While the towns of some areas, particularly those with a similar climate and a long history of Romanisation, contained houses which would not have seemed out of place in Pompeii or Herculaneum (Provence has already been mentioned[28] in this connection), others did not. Thus, it is natural that Roman houses in the eastern 'Greek' half of the Empire should follow the pattern of Hellenistic Greek houses which, as we have seen, was itself to lead in time to changes in the design of the *atrium* houses of Italy. Good examples of such Greek houses of the Roman period are to be found on the island of Delos. The House of Cleopatra and the House of Dionysos, for instance, have their rooms ranged round a colonnaded courtyard; larger houses, such as the House of the Trident, have the same basic arrangement but a so-called 'Rhodian' peristyle, where a large hall, fronted by a taller colonnade, occupies the side opposite the entrance. Town housing in other parts of the Empire was even more different; a brief survey of that of Roman Britain will serve to illustrate this variety.[29]

Sadly there is no Pompeii or Ostia in Roman Britain. Many of the towns which the Romans established in this country have, like Rome, been continuously inhabited ever since, and evidence from such sites is therefore limited. But there are exceptions to this pattern of continuous development—Calleva Atrebatum (Silchester) (fig. 5), Venta Silurum (Caerwent) (fig. 7) and Verulamium (St. Albans) immediately spring to mind—though even here the perishable nature of the building materials, particularly in houses of the early period, and the less-than-sophisticated techniques of the early excavators have not helped in the establishment of a clear picture.

The basic housing unit seems to have been the so-called 'strip' house, of which Verulamium provides some good examples. These consisted of a comparatively long, narrow building divided into five or six square or rectangular rooms. Often they were placed at right angles to the street, with the front room serving as a shop or given over to some other type of commercial activity and with the living quarters in the rooms behind; in this way several such properties could be fitted into one block. It can easily be seen how the 'corridor' house (cf. pp. 76f below) evolved from this simple structure when a corridor or verandah was added to one or both of the long sides, giving more protection against the elements and making movement from room to room easier and more pleasant.

In theory, strip or corridor houses were capable of almost indefinite extension, simply by adding on further rooms. But it would obviously be more convenient for carrying on the day-to-day business of living (as well as more practical within the confines of the customary grid-like town plan) if the extra rooms were obtained by adding on wings more or less at right angles to the original range, and this was often done on one, or more rarely on both, sides. From there, especially where there was a wing on one side only, it would be a natural stage in the evolutionary process to build a second wing at right angles to the first, giving three wings round an open courtyard, and then, after further extension, four ranged round a closed one. So evolved the so-called 'courtyard' house, which is commonly found in Roman Britain.

Such an evolutionary process need not necessarily be strictly chronological. Just as basic semi-detached houses are still being built today alongside others which have already had extensions, so new strip houses could arise alongside established courtyard ones; equally, courtyard houses could be built as entities, without having started out as something simpler. But, of course, examples where a chronological sequence can be clearly demonstrated do exist. For instance, the southernmost of the two houses discovered on the Pound Lane site in Venta Silurum (fig. 7) started life as two strip houses about 75 ft (22 m) long and 25 ft (7.4 m) wide, separated by a passage; each one had a shop at the front and four small living-rooms behind, and they were probably built around A.D. 100. However, less than fifty years later the eastern one of these was demolished and a wing containing three large living-rooms was constructed running eastwards from the rear of the western one, extending across the back part of its demolished neighbour. At about the same time or very soon afterwards an eastern range was added to give three wings in all, ranged round a courtyard which was then closed off by an entrance and colonnade. Incidentally, the northernmost of the two houses on the site seems to have been built all of a piece as a courtyard house about A.D. 200.

Occasionally we find examples of unitary courtyard houses of the so-called 'Mediterranean' type. These are much more compact than the courtyard houses just mentioned (which tend to be rather sprawling), with their rooms facing inwards on to a small colonnaded area reminiscent of the peristyle courts of Italian houses. They have been found at Glevum (Gloucester) and Camulodunum (Colchester) as well as at Venta Silurum;[30] we might suspect that the builders of such houses were Romans with military connections, since the ground plans show distinct similarities to the commandants' houses (*praetoria*) of Roman camps (cf. pp. 161f below).

The housing in Roman towns was obviously in many respects far different from that in our towns today; yet in some ways its history and development were, in broad terms, very similar. When we reflect on the extremes of housing type in Pompeii and Herculaneum, comparing, for example, the House of the Faun with the cramped accommodation over shops; when we see how the larger Pompeian house was a forceful statement of how the owner wanted his neighbours to see him; when we consider how in Ostia overcrowding and the rising value of land led to the rapid emergence of apartment blocks and how the reverse situation led, almost equally quickly, to their demise; when we note the practice of extending one's property in Roman Britain; it is then that we realise that the attitudes to, and the reactions to, the problems of housing the urban population in the Roman world were not so very different from our own.

NOTES

1. *On Architecture* 6, esp. ch. 3.

2. The etymology occurs in Servius, *On the Aeneid* 1.726. He mentions a kitchen, not a hearth-fire, but in a primitive house there was probably little difference between the two. The younger Seneca (*Letter* 44.5) writes of the '*atrium* full of smoky images [of ancestors]'; cf. in Cicero, *In Pisonem* 1.1 and Juvenal 8.8. Another definition connects the word with the Etruscan town of Atria (Varro, *On the Latin Language* 5.161). Yet another idea, that *atrium* is derived from the Greek word *aithrion*, is unlikely to be correct for so early a feature.

3. The *compluvium* also, of course, admitted light, and this must have been a considerable benefit. But the words *compluvium* and *impluvium* are both connected with the Latin word for rain (*pluvia*), which points to the equal importance of the rainwater aspect. The definitions occur in Varro, *On the Latin Language* 5.161, though there he also mentions 'space left in the middle to catch the light'.

4. 6.3.1–2.

5. See A. Wallace-Hadrill, 'The social structure of the Roman house', *Papers of the British School at Rome* (new series) 43 (1988), 64–68. He refers (p. 64) to columns as 'the hallmark of Greek public and sacred architecture' and asks 'whether associations

with public buildings did not adhere, at least at times, in their employment by the Romans'.

6. The Corinthian type in particular is reminiscent of the peristyle of the 'Greek' part of the house (see below), though the columns were more closely spaced.

7. Illustrated in A. Boethius, *Etruscan and Early Roman Architecture* (Harmondsworth 1978), fig. 89 on p. 90.

8. Some houses, such as the House of the Wooden Partition at Herculaneum (pl. 7), have solid benches in the street outside, set against the front walls on either side of the main door; these may have been for the use of clients awaiting admission.

9. Wallace-Hadrill, 'The social structure of the Roman house', 55. Elsewhere in the same paper, referring to the Roman ruling class, he writes of 'the incompatibility of public life and privacy' and 'the interpenetration of public and private life'.

10. The House of the Stags (fig. 17) also has no *tablinum* and only a small *atrium*, but, because of the different shape of the plot already referred to, the court (here surrounded by a *cryptoporticus* rather than a colonnade) opens off from one corner.

11. The dining-room at Chedworth Villa in Gloucestershire exhibits a similar arrangement. The inner (southern) area of the room, where the diners would have been, has the plainer mosaic, and is marked off by a pair of shallow responds from the northern part with its great Bacchic mosaic.

12. 6.4.

13. *Satyricon* 77.4. The whole description is interesting: 'It [the house] has got four dining-rooms [*cenationes*], twenty bedrooms, two marble colonnades, a dining-room [?] upstairs, a bedroom in which I sleep, a boudoir for this viper [his wife], and an excellent cubby-hole for the doorkeeper; the guest wing holds a hundred [?] guests'. The upstairs dining-room is included as a result of a textual emendation; 'upstairs bathroom' is another attractive suggestion. Even if the hundred-bed guest wing (itself another emendation) is a comic exaggeration, it is clear that the four dining-rooms are not in any way unusual for a man of Trimalchio's wealth and pretensions.

14. Wallace-Hadrill ('The social structure of the Roman house', p.59 and note 44) points to the conducting of imperial trials *intra cubiculum* (lit. 'within the bedroom'), the fact that Tacitus' *Dialogue on Oratory* is set in a bedroom, and several other examples. Some of these instances remind one of the formal *levée* of the French kings in the King's Bedroom at Versailles.

15. 6.3.8–10.

16. This and the other excavated houses of Vasio very closely reflect Pompeian models.

17. 2.8.20.

18. See the discussion of this topic in the Introduction, p. 3.

19. For housing in Ostia in general and for its *insulae* and later peristyle houses in particular, see R. Meiggs, *Roman Ostia,* 2nd edition (Oxford 1973), 235–62.

20. Livy 21.62.3.

21. Strabo 5.3.7 (235).

22. 2.8.17; and see references in Introduction, notes 2 and 3.

23. See F. Coarelli, *Roma* (*Guide archeologiche Laterza* 6) (Rome 1980), 37. The building appears in a brief list of surviving remains of *insulae* in Rome given in Meiggs, *Roman Ostia*, 238f.

24. Meiggs, *Roman Ostia*, 241.

25. This was, strictly speaking, not a private dwelling at all, but the headquarters of a guild (*collegium*). But it, like some other Ostian buildings such as the barracks of the fire-brigade (*vigiles*) and some of the warehouses (*horrea*), is so similar in design to some residential *insulae* that it can legitimately be mentioned in the same context. See J.B. Ward-Perkins, *Roman Imperial Architecture* (Harmondsworth 1981), 147–48, and n. 6 to ch. 6 on pp. 474–75.

26. Meiggs, *Roman Ostia*, 236–37.

27. Ward-Perkins, *Roman Imperial Architecture*, 210.

28. See p. 33 above and n. 16.

29. Most books on Roman Britain discuss houses in towns, often in the context of individual sites. Good concise accounts of housing in general are to be found in G. de la Bédoyère, *Roman Towns in Britain* (London 1992), 60–66 and 75–76.

30. See J. Wacher, *The Towns of Roman Britain* (London 1974), 110, 147 and 388.

3

Houses in the Country

JOHN PERCIVAL

To be fully a Roman, not merely in the earlier centuries of Rome's history, but up to and well beyond the time of Virgil, was to be a farmer. Those who owned no land were *capite censi*, counted by heads, mere numbers, and until the time of Marius were not officially eligible to serve in the legions. At the other end of the scale political power, in the sense of eligibility for high office, was the preserve of the landed gentry, and only under the Principate did this monopoly begin to break down, and even then in practice rather than in theory. The laws which, by barring senators from large-scale business and commerce, effectively restricted membership of the senate to landowners, may seem to us both reactionary and unnecessarily divisive; but they were consistent with a tradition which associated farming with the 'pioneer' origins of Rome, and which saw in the farmer those qualities of honest toil and pious frugality which were peculiarly Roman. Had not Romulus himself been raised in a shepherd's hut, Cincinnatus called from his plough to lead Rome against the Aequi, and was it not from agriculture (as Cato claimed) that Rome derived her best men and her best soldiers?[1]

More narrowly, and more significantly for our present concern, the importance of the identification of senators with landowners was that it ensured that land remained an attractive investment, rather than declining by comparison with the richer and faster gains to be acquired from the exploitation of Rome's growing Empire. Land was not only essential for the aspiring senator, but was desirable also for those who, though not aiming for the traditional positions of power, were anxious to achieve a measure of social respectability and status. For them the ownership of landed estates remained, and would long continue to be, the main (perhaps the sole) prerequisite. Other factors will have helped, no doubt, to keep the market in land buoyant: the requirements of the armies in terms of provisioning will have provided, for Italy of the later Republic as for the provinces in the early Principate, a major stimulus to agricultural production and therefore to the attractiveness of land as a source of income.[2] The availability of cheap labour, in the form of slaves, will have provided a stimulus of another kind, and the effects of capitalist farming on all aspects of life in the centuries before and after Augustus are well documented. But, whatever the primary cause may have been, it was to the landowner that Rome, in this central period at least, can be said to have belonged.

And so it is that, when we are first able to study houses in the country at close quarters, in Italy of the last two centuries B.C., what strikes us is not an air of Romantic rusticity or well-cushioned comfort so much as one of work and efficient production. It is there most obviously in the manuals of Cato and Varro; it is there also in the varied pronouncements and passing references of Cicero; and it is even there in the description of his estate by Horace, for whom the five tenant farmers and their families are as much worthy of mention as are the amenities of the house itself.[3] For such people (though less, perhaps, for Horace than for the others) the ownership of land was a primary concern and not a secondary one: that is, it was not a question of estates and country houses being something on which a wealthy man could spend his money, but rather that those estates and houses were the very basis, not only of his wealth, but of the status that went with it. By the same token, though undoubtedly a retreat in some senses, they were not a retreat from 'real' life; on the contrary, 'real' life was represented by them and by the work which went on within and around them.

A similar picture is offered by the growing number of excavated sites from this same late Republican period: however comfortable a house may be, and however much it may have been designed as a little bit of the town in the country, the chances are that its role as a working farm will be just as much in evidence. The Roman villa (for this is what we are here concerned with) is commonly considered under a number of categories: the working farm, the country residence with farming associated, the country retreat for rest and recuperation, the seat of luxury and pleasure.[4] All of these can be exemplified at most periods and in most parts of the Empire, but it is the link with practical farming that remains most constant and central. There were, of course, exceptional areas and exceptional periods: one thinks immediately of Italy in the first century A.D., when a scramble for country estates as seats of leisure and luxury was indulged in by 'the pleasure seekers, the moody recluses and the profiteers',[5] and when the passion for lavish seaside villas provided for poets and moralists a ready example of ostentatious self-indulgence. There were signs of this much earlier: Varro deplored a tendency to give greater attention to the residential aspects of villas than to their working buildings, and Cicero refers to landowners who used the income from their working estates to finance expenditure on seaside houses.[6] But taking the Empire as a whole, it is really only in a minority of cases, where the richest houses merge into what would more properly be called palaces, that the link is broken and the close association with the countryside as a context of work and the production (rather than the consumption) of wealth abandoned.

The point is neatly illustrated by Vitruvius. Having dealt with town houses in the first part of his sixth book, he says that the principles there outlined will apply equally to houses in the country, except that the relative positioning of atrium and peristyle will differ; and he then goes on to deal with farmhouses (*aedificia rustica*, as opposed to *urbana*), concentrating on animal quarters, storerooms, kitchens and so on. The implication, certainly, is that country houses may be no less luxurious than town ones; but there is a clear implication also that in the country the 'urban' and 'rustic' buildings, though possibly separate, are normally closely associated. And the point is made very clearly a little later, when he says that if a degree of refinement in farmhouses is desired, the principles set out for town houses can apply, 'provided that there is nothing in such buildings to interfere with their usefulness on a farm'.[7]

As an example of how this looked on the ground the San Rocco villa at Francolise in northern Campania can hardly be bettered.[8] The first house here was built c.100–90 B.C., and consisted of a relatively modest residence with farm buildings adjoining it and on a lower terrace. Later, perhaps around 50 B.C., the residential part was remodelled and made more private and more comfortable; additional bedrooms were provided and new mosaic pavements installed. By now we have a house in which a successful farmer and his family could have lived on a permanent basis, or which could perhaps have been used for regular visits or as a summer residence by someone from a nearby town. The farm buildings of this period have been largely obliterated by later developments, but they contained what appear to be two small threshing floors, a well and water cistern, and provision for storage. A little later still, it is thought around 30 B.C., the whole site was transformed (fig. 22). A large and impressive residence, with numerous rooms surrounding a central peristyle, now covered the whole of the original area. Every room, including the peristyle, was provided either with a mosaic or with a pavement in *opus signinum*, and great care was shown in co-ordinating these with each

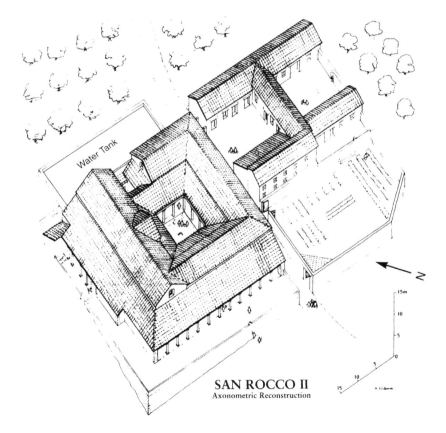

SAN ROCCO II
Axonometric Reconstruction

Fig. 22: Francolise, Italy: San Rocco villa. Restored axonometric plan of the Period II villa, early first century A.D.

other and with the surviving pavements of the earlier house. Attention
was also given to the outward appearance of the house, to the way in
which it blended into the landscape and to its aspects when approached
from various directions. Clearly, in Vitruvian terms, a need has been felt
for a degree of refinement, and the principles of symmetry appropriate to
a town house have been duly applied. But equally, the site remains
a farm, and its usefulness as such is certainly not interfered with.
Adjoining the residence on its eastern side, and separated only by a
central access road, there are now extensive work buildings, arranged
around a pair of courtyards, and to the south of them a walled garden.
The working part of the establishment now includes what appear to be
stables, another threshing floor, and extensive living quarters, presumably for staff. To the north of both this and the residential part there
are huge cisterns for collecting and storing water; and for all its luxury
and architectural refinement the site is still a working farm, and an
efficient and carefully planned one at that. Further modifications in the
mid-first century A.D. continue the pattern: there is a new bath house for
the residence, and a tile kiln and olive processing unit are established in
the work buildings. The two elements of house and farm, leisure and
work, remain closely linked and interdependent.

It is in such establishments, one must suppose, that Cicero will have
stayed in his periods away from Rome, and from which he will have
written his letters and maintained contact with the political and social
life of the city. For him, and for others of his class and interests, they will
have served sometimes as staging posts on longer journeys and
sometimes as places to stay for weeks on end, for writing the next book
or simply to get away from a political situation that had become uncom-
fortable. For his purposes, no doubt, there will have been a need for a
degree of comfort, as well as extensive accommodation for his family
and friends, for servants and assistants of various kinds, and for his
books and papers; and certainly it is to these kinds of people and these
kinds of amenities that he normally refers when writing from or about
his houses in the country. But the estates of which those houses are a
part, and the agricultural investment of which they are the centre, are
never far from his thoughts. There are numerous letters in which he
discusses the purchase of this or that property, or asks for help in finding
property in this or that area; and others in which he refers to matters
needing attention or tours of inspection that need to be made. Cicero,
one has to assume, is at the top of the market, and more involved than
anyone in the life of the city; and if the practical, business side of country

living is high on his list of priorities it will have been even higher on that of more 'normal' or more 'average' people.

To the San Rocco villa, which we used as the typical late Republican house, could be added a number of other examples, differing in size and plan and in the level of luxury, but similar in combining the comfortable residence with the working farm. Not far from San Rocco, at Posto in the same district of Francolise,[9] a villa established between 100 and 80 B.C. went through at least three building phases before gradually falling into disuse some time in the latter part of the second century A.D. (fig. 23). Here the buildings were grouped around a single courtyard, with less in the way of comfort and refinement and a less clear distinction between the residential and the working areas; one thinks, perhaps, of a

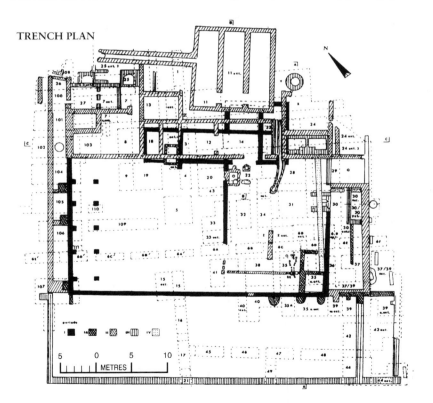

Fig. 23: Francolise, Posto villa. Overall plan of the excavations, showing the main building periods.

permanently resident farming family rather than of one which came and went from season to season. Between them, this and the San Rocco house provide us with an idea of the medium range, as it were, of late Republican villas. Below them in luxury are sites such as the Sambuco villa at San Giovenale in Etruria, which is not much more than a well-appointed farm cottage,[10] or the regularly illustrated site at Boscoreale, a mile or two north of Pompeii,[11] which is larger and more carefully planned but consists almost entirely of working areas with just one small corner providing living accommodation. Higher up the scale in terms of amenities are several of the other sites in the Campanian region, some of them essentially suburban to Pompeii itself and others approaching in lavishness the seaside houses already referred to. Attention in this area has tended to concentrate on the richer sites, and it is in other parts of Italy that recent excavation has provided more representative examples.

For all of these houses, from the richest and most lavishly appointed down to the comparatively modest, the indispensable guide is the younger Pliny, whose letters contain numerous references to his own and his friends' properties, to the activities associated with them and to their role in the economic and social life of their owners. His own villas, of course, were mostly at the more prosperous end of the market, and included the seaside house of Laurentum, near Ostia, as well as a number of houses along the shores of Lake Como. The famous description of Laurentum,[12] so detailed that plans and models of it have been constructed, concentrates almost entirely on its role as a residence; the colonnades, dining-rooms, baths, library and so on are described in terms of their overall layout and design, and the emphasis throughout is on the variety of provision for winter and summer conditions, entertaining friends or private relaxation and study, and of vistas of sea and shoreline. There is a garden, with fruit trees, and enough land to provide the house with its everyday needs. But there is little indication that it is anything other than a place to get away to and relax in, the kind of place that in another letter he calls a *pinguis secessus*, 'a comfortable retreat' where you can bury yourself in your books. Indeed, he says as much to another friend: '*nihil quidem ibi possideo praeter tectum et hortum statimque harenas*', ('all I have there is the house and garden and the adjacent beach').[13] In an equally lengthy description of another of his houses in Tuscany, there is the same emphasis on the residence itself, but the description begins with references to meadows and cornfields and some comments on the local soil, suggesting at least that there was rather more in the way of farming here than at Laurentum.[14]

A hint as to his real priorities, or at least what he took to be the priorities of members of his social circle, is provided in a letter in which he asks for help in finding a property for his friend Suetonius; what he wants, he says, is 'easy access to Rome, good communications, a modest house, and sufficient land for him to enjoy without taking up too much of his time'.[15] 'Enjoying' the land meant not only relaxing in rural surroundings but enjoying the income it brought, and when it comes to buying properties for himself Pliny (as one would expect from one of the leading financial experts of his day) is shrewd and calculating. The letter in which he asks advice about buying the estate adjoining one of his own is devoted entirely to estimates of what it would cost to get it back into working order, how its management could be integrated with his existing property, and how the asking price related to its market value.[16] In this case the residences are of less importance; he will furnish one and merely keep the other in reasonable repair. The steward will look after them, and the foreman will handle the workforce. What we are concerned with here is an investment, with land and the houses upon them as a source of income. That income may go partly to pay for more comfortable and less productive houses elsewhere, but they are the bonus; here is where the work is done, and where time has to be spent on serious planning.

We do not, unfortunately, have the writings of provincial Plinys to provide us with similar information about houses in Spain or Gaul or Britain (though we can look forward to people not unlike him rather later on). One has to assume, however, that the pattern he illustrates for first-century Italy was essentially the pattern at least throughout the developed and Romanised parts of the Empire. With the spread of the Roman peace throughout the provinces, the country house, along with the language, the adoption of Roman dress, and civic amenities, was rapidly adopted as a mark of Romanisation among the provincial well-to-do. Agricola's famous encouragement to the people of Britain to become Roman is essentially an exhortation to adopt a town-based way of life, and in this context *aedes* probably means town houses rather than country villas.[17] But villas were certainly part of the early Romanisation of Britain, and there is some evidence that in south-east Britain at least the changes in the countryside pre-dated those in the towns.[18] It is fair to say, indeed, that it was in the western provinces generally that the villa developed most successfully and evolved into the widest range of designs; and part of the reason may well have been the reluctance of the peoples of the west to abandon their traditional non-urban culture. Here, perhaps, in a fuller sense than in Italy, the country, and country living, sustained the city rather than vice versa.

Whatever the precise relationship, however (and there were no doubt regional variations that we may one day be able to detect and illustrate), it was a symbiotic one both in its origins and early development and in its later, established form. The distribution of villas, as has long been recognised, is closely related to that of towns, and to the communication network (primarily the roads but also the rivers) which linked them all together. There was an economic relationship between the two in terms of markets; and to judge from the facilities and amenities regularly to be found in the villas there was a social relationship also. As in Italy, for the well-to-do at least, town and country represented alternative and complementary bases of activity for what was largely the same class of people. The villas around Cirencester, say, or Toulouse or Trier will have belonged to people for whom life in both town and country was normal and familiar, whether they were councillors or businessmen with estates for pleasure and profit or full-time farmers who came up to town to buy and sell and keep in touch with the world. They would, one supposes, have understood, and been understood by, both Pliny and Cicero, and more readily still by people less distracted than they were by their involvement in public life.

Throughout the provinces the first villas appear within a generation or two of the establishment of peaceful conditions, and are for the most part very modest houses rather than fully developed villas of the Italian type. Examples of the latter can certainly be found, particularly in such areas as Spain and southern Gaul where the Roman presence came early and where there was already a Romanised cultural base on which colonial immigrants from Italy could quickly build. One thinks in this connection of Chiragan,[19] perhaps, or La Cocosa, near Badajoz (fig. 24),[20] both of which were established at an early date and are recognisably Italian in their overall design. In Britain such examples are more rare, and a site such as Lullingstone, which has sometimes been claimed as belonging to a Roman official,[21] is already built to a plan which we would regard not entirely as Italian but rather as north-European with some Italian influence (fig. 25). Whatever their style, however, it was probably such officials or immigrants who were responsible for these early villas, and they are to be seen essentially as importations, and as models, perhaps, of what was possible for the local gentry. It is among these local people, one assumes, that we should look for the owners of the much less sophisticated houses that are more common in these

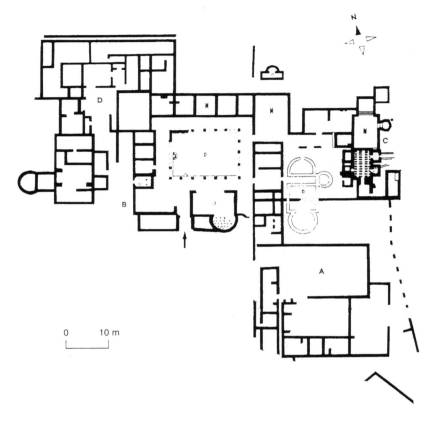

Fig. 24: Badajoz, Spain: La Cocosa villa. Main residential area of the peristyle villa.

earliest periods. For them, perhaps, they will have represented an adoption of the outward trappings of Roman-ness without at this stage implying (or not necessarily) an abandonment in any real sense of their native culture. The earliest phases of sites such as Lockleys in Hertfordshire,[22] Brixworth in Northamptonshire[23] or Mayen in the Rhineland[24] are 'Roman' to an extent in their building design, with their neatly rectangular plans and their stone-built wall foundations; but they are 'native' still in their smallness and in their emphasis (most noticeable in continental examples) on a single hall-like central room with its implications of communal living. Gradually the separate rooms become more numerous, for eating, sleeping and for separating out the activities of

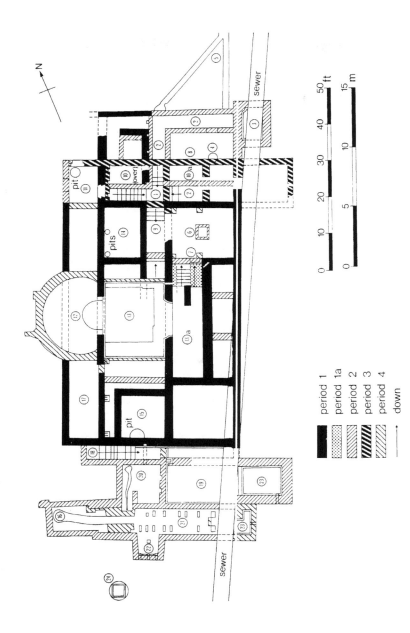

period 1
period 1a
period 2
period 3
period 4
down

Fig. 25: The villa at Lullingstone, Kent.

work and pleasure; and the plans become more complex and less completely utilitarian. Simple porches and porticoes appear, and in due course the acquisition of baths, heated rooms, painted wall plaster and mosaic pavements mark the rapid stages towards a fully Roman lifestyle. One needs to be cautious, no doubt, in using physical amenities as an indication of cultural attitudes; the point at which the trappings of Roman-ness can be taken as evidence for a full adoption and assimilation of Roman culture is not easy to identify, and some have questioned whether, in large areas of the Empire, the point was ever really reached.[25] But in general terms, and certainly without too close a concern with semantics, the notion of the villa as one of the major indicators of Romanisation is clearly valid and helpful.

Complete examples of the very earliest Romanised houses are not as readily available as one would wish, mainly because they were regularly obliterated by, or incorporated in, their own later expansions and developments. Of their later, more developed phases we have, on the other hand, examples literally in their hundreds from all of the major provinces, and the problem is essentially where to begin and how in a relatively short account to give some idea both of their variety and of what gives them their common identity. The normal solution is to classify them in terms of their ground plans, and this has a number of advantages. The first is that in spite of what seems to be, and indeed is, a very rich variety of plans, they can in fact be reduced to quite a small number of basic types. Second, these types are not entirely separate from one another; the most common of them can be linked in the sense that they can be seen as evolving from one another, not only in theory but often in practice on an individual site. And third (though here one has to be careful not to over-simplify) the types can be related to economic and social classes and categories.

The outlines of the scheme were set out by Collingwood in the 1930s, and scholars since then have done little more than add a number of refinements and sub-types, usually to accommodate the examples from their own particular area.[26] Central to Collingwood's scheme was what he called the corridor villa, which sometimes included a corridor in the true sense of a passageway linking one or more rooms, but more often denoted a house with a simple portico along its front, usually open on its outer side and with a lean-to roof. This simple refinement was seen by him, and by contemporary scholars on the Continent, as a significant indication of Romanising tendencies, partly in the sense that it was a feature that was not wholly practical and essential, but also in that its origins seemed to be in the shops and smaller craftsmen's houses of Roman towns. In German the type came to be known as a *Portikusvilla*, and in French a villa *à galerie-façade*, both of them rather more accurate terms than 'corridor', and Mayen, to which we have already referred (p. 74), has served as the standard example of the type in the majority of the textbooks. The portico, by presenting a facade to someone approaching the house, invited further development, and this in the great majority of cases took the form of two rooms placed symmetrically at each end of it. The use to which these rooms were put is not always clear, though it seems unlikely that they were ever regarded as the most important rooms in the house; this role tended to be taken by a more centrally placed room which can be seen either as the successor of the single hall-like room in the earliest examples or as a main reception room in a Roman sense. The corner rooms will probably have had different roles in different houses, and in some cases they are small enough to suggest that they may even have been thought of first as part of the overall design and only later in terms of their specific function.

Whatever the details of its origin and rationale, however, the 'corridor' villa is by far the most common type, at least so far as the western provinces of the Empire are concerned, and literally hundreds of examples of it can be identified from north Africa to Yorkshire and from Portugal to Bavaria. One site can happily stand as representative for all of them, and for Britain the house at Gadebridge Park, near Hemel Hempstead in Hertfordshire (fig. 26), will do as well as any other.[27]

Like a number of other sites in this part of Britain, the house here seems to have begun about three-quarters of the way through the first century with a timber phase, the plan of which has been destroyed by later developments. At this stage the only stone-built feature is a small bath house, built for obvious safety reasons at some distance from the main dwelling. It is not until a century later, in the late Antonine period, that a recognisable villa appears, in the form of a stone-built 'corridor' house, 41.5 x 24 m, comprising some eight rooms with intervening passageways, and a portico or verandah extending all around it rather than merely along the front. Already, that is, the basic type is being improved upon, and there is a further refinement in that the wing rooms at each end of the main facade are somewhat extended; indeed, the one at the south-eastern corner is the largest in the house, and is built on two levels, the lower level being a semi-basement similar to those more commonly seen on the Continent.

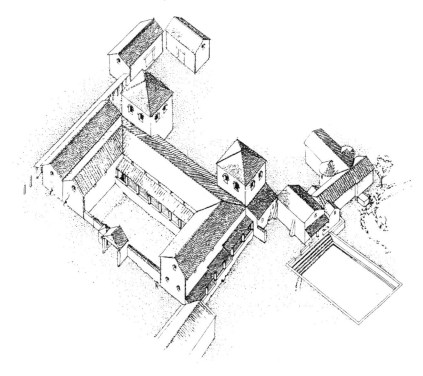

Fig. 26: Gadebridge Park, Hertfordshire. Reconstruction drawing of villa in Period 6 (fourth century A.D.).

The appearance at this date of a new house, apparently planned and built in a single operation rather than evolving gradually, and occupying the site of the (presumably demolished) earlier dwelling, suggests a change of ownership and some degree of wealth. It would be wrong, however, to see it as anything other than a working farm. As the excavators observe, the interior was very plain, with *opus signinum* floors and mainly undecorated plaster on the walls; none of the rooms can confidently be identified as a dining-room. There are sufficient rooms, no doubt, to separate the accommodation of the owner's family from that of his servants, but the possibility that the 'basement' room was used as a stable should make us wary of assuming that here was a place of leisure, or even of much comfort. This was to come in later, fourth-century, phases, when the baths were greatly extended and a large swimming-pool was added to them; but in these early stages the emphasis is definitely upon work rather than play.

What the Gadebridge Park site shows is that the 'corridor' type of house, though at first sight fairly simple and even rather constraining in its layout, was in fact much more flexible than would appear, partly in that it could be elaborated within its basic plan, and partly in that it could naturally evolve into grander and more extended types. One fairly obvious elaboration (more common, as it happens, than the all-round portico here) was to repeat the portico and balancing corner rooms on the rear as well as the front of the house, so improving its appearance when approached from either direction and also perhaps providing alternative amenities appropriate to the different seasons of the year. Such, for example, is the plan of Maubeuge in northern France[28] or Hambledon in Buckinghamshire.[29] Another development, favoured particularly on the Continent, was greatly to elongate the plan, so that to someone approaching the house it would appear to be much larger than it actually was. A good example of this is Hosté in Belgium,[30] which has a facade extending over 150 m, but is not much more than 20 m deep from front to back (fig. 27). In some ways these apparently rather exaggerated plans are not unlike some of the Italian seaside villas, with their long covered porticoes extending along the shoreline. Seen in this way, Hosté is similar to (say) the villa at Nennig in north Germany,[31] except that here the colonnade (some 250 m in length) is an added, and entirely separate, feature rather than being incorporated in the house's overall plan.

More commonly the basic plan is extended, not by stretching the facade, but by developing one or both of the corner rooms into wings in their own right. Collingwood's example of this was the villa at Box, near Bath in Wiltshire,[32] but, as we saw, it was already beginning to happen at Gadebridge Park, and for more obvious examples one might point also to Witcombe in Gloucestershire,[33] or Weitersbach near Trier (fig. 28).[34] Once this has been done, of course, the space enclosed within the wings and the main facade can be developed into a garden or courtyard and ultimately enclosed altogether. Thus the 'winged corridor' villa (to continue with Collingwood's terminology) develops naturally into the 'courtyard villa', as happens briefly in a late second- or early third-century phase at Gadebridge Park and more permanently at North Leigh in Oxfordshire,[35] or Pitney in Somerset.[36] In some cases all four sides are 'wings' in the true sense of being suites of rooms, but more frequently the buildings are simply arranged around a central yard and perhaps

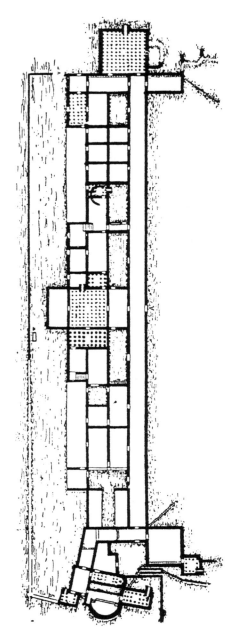

Fig. 27: The villa at Hosté, Brabant, Belgium.

Plate 1: Part of a model of City of Rome, looking north. In foreground, buildings on Mons Caelius; then a branch of the Aqua Claudia leading to the Palatine (to left); above and to right of the Colosseum, the Baths of Trajan covering a wing of Nero's Domus Aurea; upper right, the Esquiline; upper left, the crowded residential area of the Subura.

Plate 2: Thamugadi: aerial view, looking north. The square blocks of the original *colonia* can be seen in the upper right section of the photograph.

Plate 3: Pompeii: view from city wall along Via di Mercurio.

Plate 4: A street in Ostia.

Plate 5: Pompeii: street fountain.

Plate 6: Pompeii: water pipes.

Plate 7: Herculaneum: House of the
Wooden Partition, facade.

Plate 8: Pompeii, House of the Impluvium.

Plate 9: Herculaneum: House of the Wooden Partition, atrium.

Plate 10: Pompeii: House of Epidius Rufus.

Plate 11: Pompeii: House of the Vettii, peristyle and garden.

Plate 12: Pompeii: House of the Vettii, kitchen.

Plate 13: Herculaneum: Trellis House.

Plate 14: Ostia: House of Diana.

Plate 15: Rome: Domus Aurea, octagon room.

Plate 16: Sirmio: early Imperial villa, *cryptoporticus* overlooking Lake Garda.

Plate 17: Rome: Domitian's palace, restoration by G. Tognetti (1900).

Plate 18: Rome: Domus Flavia, *triclinium*.

Plate 19: Hadrian's Villa, 'Canopus'.

Plate 20: Hadrian's Villa, island pavilion ('Maritime Theatre').

Plate 21: Split: Diocletian's palace, 'Peristyle'.

Plate 22: The view from the terrace of the Temple of Venus Cnidia at Hadrian's Villa, towards Tivoli.

Plate 23: One wall of Livia's garden-room, from the villa *Ad Gallinas Albas* at Prima Porta.

Plate 24: Caerleon, Prysg Field: legionary barrack—general view.

Plate 25: Caerleon, Prysg Field: legionary barrack—detail of centurion's quarters.

Plate 26: Caerleon, Prysg Field: legionary barrack—detail of *contubernium* with fortress rampart and centurial ovens in the background.

Plate 27: Chesters: auxiliary barracks—view of facing pair of barracks looking towards the decurions' quarters.

Plate 28: Chesters: auxiliary barrack—detail of *contubernium* with stone paving.

Plate 29: Poltross Burn, Hadrian's Wall: Milecastle barrack.

Plate 30: Saalburgmuseum, Bad Homburg: reconstruction of auxiliary barracks.

linked by an enclosing wall. The next and final stage in the development
is the addition of a second courtyard from which this first one is
approached; there are a few examples of this in Britain, but many more
on the Continent, and on most such sites the result of the arrangement
(and presumably the intention behind it) is further to separate out the
residential part of the establishment from the working part. As you
approach the house, you pass first into what is essentially a farmyard,

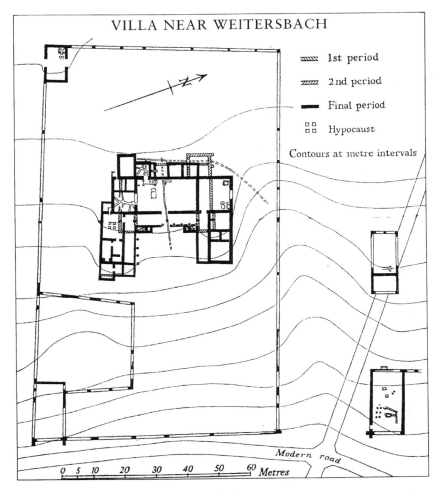

Fig. 28: Weitersbach villa, Germany. General plan.

albeit enclosed by well-ordered, even elegant ranges of buildings; and beyond this you go through a second gateway to enter a usually smaller courtyard, perhaps with trees and ornamental gardens, which is at the heart of the residence itself. The area where houses of this type occur most frequently, or at least where they are most available for examination now, is in the Somme basin of northern France, where literally

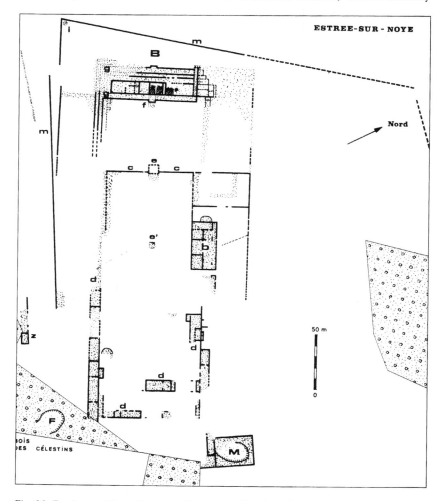

Fig. 29: Estrées-sur-Noye (Somme), France. A plan, based on air photography, of the double-courtyard villa.

scores of examples have been revealed by aerial survey.[37] The site at Estrées-sur-Noye (Somme)[38] is typical of these (fig. 29), and Bignor in Sussex[39] provides a parallel example from Britain.

What is interesting about this sequence of plans, if we are right in seeing it as such, is that it is as much 'provincial' as 'Roman' in character. That is to say, if we take at any rate the western provinces of the Empire as a whole, they did not simply take over the designs of Italian country houses and adapt them; rather, they evolved designs of their own. Published plans of Italian villas are still not as numerous as one would wish, but taken as a collection they do not in any sense illustrate the sequence just described. Indeed, one is hard pressed to find a single example of any of the types that we have identified as being standard in Britain, Gaul and elsewhere. In the country, it would appear, what mainly dictated design was consideration of locality, climate and practical use at least as much as a desire for Roman-ness for its own sake. There are examples in the provinces of what one could describe as 'Italian' houses; we have referred to some of them already as being among the earliest examples, built (one assumes) by expatriate officials or businessmen to recreate the life to which they were accustomed. There were others too, throughout the period of the Empire, designed and built around a central peristyle and looking inwards to a more enclosed and private establishment not very different from the town houses of Pompeii as well as the houses in the surrounding countryside. Such, for example, are Montmaurin[40] or Lalonquette (fig. 30)[41] in south-west France, or the so-called 'Villa Fortunatus' in Fraga, Spain.[42] But the fact that examples of this type are predominantly in Spain and southern Gaul confirms the view that they are essentially Mediterranean in concept, and that they occur here not least because they are appropriate to the climate and more practicable than they would be further north.

At the other end of the cultural scale, as it were, and peculiarly British in its distribution, is the type of building that used to be called 'basilican' but is now more accurately (if more prosaically) referred to as an aisled house.[43] This is a simple rectangular structure, divided internally by two rows of posts or columns into what one can call a nave and side aisles, and in many cases subdivided into smaller rooms within this overall plan. It frequently appears as a subsidiary building within a larger complex, the most striking example being its multiple occurrence at Winterton in Lincolnshire,[44] but there are cases (such as Stroud in Hampshire)[45] where it seems to exist as a house in its own right, and for this reason it tends to be added to the formal typology, even by

continental scholars, for whom it is something of a rarity. Whatever its
significance, however, and whatever its origins, it would seem to be a
relatively primitive type, clearly 'native' rather than 'Roman' in its
influences, and to this extent not central to our present concern.

It should perhaps be said that the typology here outlined does not,
by any means, cover all the houses that have been discovered. In many
cases, one suspects, additions and reconstructions over a lengthy period
have obliterated what began as a recognisable type. In others, because of

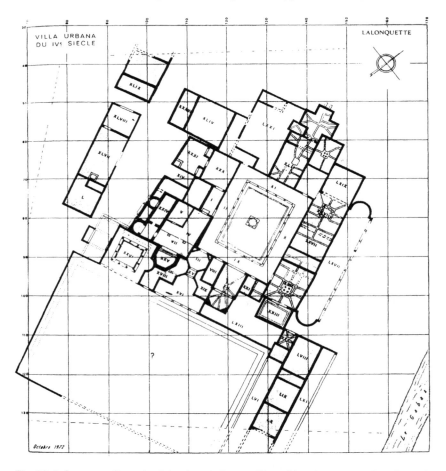

Fig. 30: Lalonquette (Pyrenées-Atlantiques), France. Plan of fourth-century villa. The grid
is of 10-metre squares.

partial excavation or partial destruction of the site by later development, the plan as a whole is not identifiable and we need to postpone judgement. But there are clearly cases where the layout is the result of planning for specific tastes and requirements rather than of the influence of received ideas and fashions; nor, considering the size of the Empire and the area over which villas extended, should this be at all surprising. Nevertheless, the percentage of sites which either fall under, or can be interpreted in terms of, one of the main types is sufficiently high to justify the continued use of the typology overall as a guide, provided always that the interpretation goes further than this and we are not content merely to apply the appropriate label.

The range of these houses, in terms of size alone, is enormous, from (say) the 'cottage' at Frilford in Berkshire[46] to the vast establishment at Chiragan, where the residential part alone extends over some 2.5 ha. Indeed, apart from the term villa as being applicable to all of them, and the fact that they are all 'houses in the country', one is tempted at times to ask whether there is anything significant that they have in common. There is a similar range in the degree of luxury and the level of their amenities, from the simple farmsteads where humans and animals are at best in separate rooms rather than separate buildings, and where everything is plain and functional, to the almost palatial mansions where no expense is spared either on physical comfort or visual splendour. This being said, it is really quite remarkable how common are the amenities which, one has to assume, will have involved both considerable expense and a certain level of expertise: amenities such as baths and central heating systems, mosaic pavements and painted wall plaster, which (significantly) are what the average visitor expects to see and which in the popular mind are what, essentially, a villa is.

We know most, perhaps, about the manufacture of mosaics, though even here there are no figures available regarding relative cost. It now seems fairly clear, from studies made in Britain, France and north Africa, that the better quality pavements were the work of craftsmen, based presumably in the towns, who travelled out to the sites to carry out specific orders.[47] 'Schools' of mosaicists is perhaps too grand a word, but there are certainly a number of workshops, or groups of workshops with a common style, which can be identified. This, no doubt, is the luxury end of the market, but the installation of even a small pavement of simple design would be a craftsman's job. Similar considerations, one assumes, would apply to wall decorations, whether in fresco or patterned marble, as well as to bath blocks, central heating systems and ornamental gardens. The effect of these and other refinements is to produce what one can only describe as an impression of great confidence on the part of the houses' owners. These, even at a relatively modest level, are establishments on which there has been considerable capital outlay; and although, as we know, they were to go through periods of decline and depression, they are in their way as striking an image of Roman permanence as are the more obvious monuments of the towns. They were, after all, undefended. At the end of the Empire, it is true, one can point to examples which look as though they have been built with security in mind, and to some which may actually have been fortified;[48] but the great majority, for most of the time, were open and in open country, and, misplaced as the confidence may have been at certain periods, it is nevertheless impressive.

Their history is essentially that of the Empire itself. As we have already noted, they followed, within a generation or two, the establishment of Roman authority in a given area, and developed rapidly during the peace and prosperity of the first and second centuries A.D. In Gaul, where the earliest (southern) examples began in the late Republic, it was in the Antonine period that their numbers were greatest and the quality of their design and construction most evident. In Britain, where the appropriate conditions were not available until the turn of the first century, their progress was rather slower, and when the troubles of the third century intervened they were still some way behind their counterparts on the Continent. The third century saw a decline in the villa as in most other aspects of Roman life, and there is abundant evidence, from all of the western provinces, of dilapidation, abandonment and destruction in both smaller and larger houses. Many which had flourished for a century or more went out of use and were not reoccupied, and the revival, when it came, was uneven both in its distribution and in the quality of its building and design. Houses tended to be less luxurious, and there was a noticeable shift from comfort towards more working establishments. Only here and there can one see a revival in the truest sense, with new houses rivalling or even surpassing those which had existed before the collapse. In south-west Gaul, around the late Imperial capital at Trier, and most strikingly in Britain, there is a fourth-century resurgence of villas, reflecting perhaps a widening of the gap between rich and poor and the opportunities now open to the former of accumulating land on a grander scale than before.

There are indications, indeed, that these landed gentry, many of them (one suspects) senatorial and enjoying the privileges and exemptions appropriate to their class, were able to survive the invasions and anarchy of the late fourth century and to continue, albeit with some adjustments, well into the fifth. In Britain, admittedly, where the early withdrawal of the legions and the persistent pressures of Saxons and others brought an 'end' to the Empire which was more sudden and more fundamental, survival is likely to have been the exception rather than the rule. But on the other side of the Channel, and particularly in the area of southern and south-western Gaul already referred to, the changes were much less marked. Well into the century, with Gothic and Burgundian kingdoms well established in the former Roman provinces, and 'Roman' areas in the north being rapidly absorbed by the advancing Franks, Sidonius Apollinaris, senator and bishop, was occupying in the traditional style his villa at Avitacum, writing about it to his equally comfortable friends, and describing a world which, though subject to strains and inconveniences, was still recognisably Roman.[49] In recent years the re-dating by French scholars of mosaic pavements has led to the likelihood that many of the great villas of this part of Gaul were still flourishing not only in Sidonius' day but later still, and there are even signs that a taste for them and for the life they offered was being acquired by the new Germanic aristocracy.[50] The evidence we have is confined to the larger and more luxurious houses (that of Séviac, at Montréal (Gers) is a good example),[51] and there is a visible change in their character as compared with earlier sites. They are now more 'public' in appearance, with grand entrances and a design which seems intended primarily to impress the visitor. They have the look of official residences rather than of private houses, and if, as seems likely, they stood in relative isolation, no longer associated with other, more modest villas but with peasant dwellings of a humbler kind, they represent a social structure and pattern of power which has already a somewhat 'medieval' feel.

To go further in time would be to extend, in too speculative a manner, a history which has already lasted for more than six centuries. With the villa, as with so many things Roman, one has to beware of generalisation, and of implying, if not actually assuming, that changes from one century to another were less than radical. It may appear on the surface that Sidonius in the mid-fifth century could relate without difficulty to Pliny in the late first century; and so, on a literary level, he certainly could. But their worlds, whether physical, political, social or ideological, were different, and so were they; and houses are an extension of people rather than vice versa. This being said, the persistence of the country house as a distinctive part of Roman life is still very striking, and there is a real sense in which Rome's history can be told and illustrated by it alone. 'Villa', said Collingwood, 'means farm',[52] and so it did; nor should the link between the house and the land be forgotten. But it was more than a farm, and had this not been so the justification for a chapter devoted to it would have been (to say the least) less strong. It was, very simply, a way of life, a part of the culture, and it is as such, rather than simply as bricks and mortar, that it has to be seen.

NOTES

1. *De agri cultura*, praef. 4.

2. A.L.F. Rivet, *The Roman Villa in Britain* (London 1969), 198–200.

3. *Epistles* 1.14.1–5.

4. See, for example, A.G. McKay, *Houses, Villas and Palaces in the Roman World* (London 1975).

5. Id., 115.

6. *De lege agraria* 2.78.

7. *De architectura* 6.6.5.

8. M. Aylwin Cotton and Guy P.R. Métraux, *The San Rocco Villa at Francolise* (British School at Rome 1985).

9. M. Aylwin Cotton, *The Late Republican Villa at Posto, Francolise* (British School at Rome 1979).

10. McKay, *Houses, Villas and Palaces*, 103–4.

11. Id., 107–8.

12. *Letters*, 2.17.

13. *Letters*, 4.6; the *pinguis secessus* is in 1.3.3.

14. *Letters*, 5.6.

15. *Letters*, 1.24.

16. *Letters*, 3.19.

17. Tacitus, *Agricola* 21.1.

18. K. Branigan, *Town and Country. Verulamium and the Roman Chilterns* (Bourne End 1973), 42–48.

19. L. Joulin, *Les établissements gallo-romaines de la plaine de Martes-Tolosanes* (Paris 1901); cf. A. Grenier, *Manuel d'archéologie gallo-romaine* 2 (1934), 832–37.

20. J. de C. Serra Rafols, *La villa romana de la dehesa de la Cocosa* (Badajoz 1952); A. Garcia y Bellido, *Archivo Español de Archeologia* 26 (1953), 207–13; cf. J.G. Gorges, *Les villas hispano-romaines* (Paris 1979), 189–90, with Pl. XLIII.

21. G.W. Meates, *The Lullingstone Roman Villa* 1 (Kent Archaeological Society 1979), 24.

22. J.B. Ward-Perkins, 'The Roman Villa at Lockleys, Welwyn', *Antiquaries Journal* 18 (1938), 339–76.

23. P.J. Woods, *Brixworth Excavations* 1 (1972).

24. F. Oelmann and H. Mylius, *Bonner Jahrbücher* 133 (1928), 51–152; cf. A. Grenier, *Manuel d'archéologie gallo-romaine* 2 (1934), 784–95.

25. J.T. Smith, 'Villas as a key to social structure', in Malcolm Todd (ed.), *Studies in the Romano-British Villa* (Leicester University Press, 1978), 149–85; id., 'Villa plans and social structure in Britain and Gaul', *Caesarodunum* 17 (1982), 321–36.

26. R.G. Collingwood, *The Archaeology of Roman Britain* (London 1930).

27. David S. Neal, *The Excavation of the Roman Villa in Gadebridge Park, Hemel Hempstead 1963–8* (London 1974).

28. *Gallia* 35 (1977), 285–86.

29. A.H. Cocks, 'A Romano-British Homestead in the Hambledon Valley, Bucks.', *Archaeologia* 71 (1921), 141–98.

30. *Annales de la Société archéologique de Bruxelles* 19 (1905), 303f.

31. E.M. Wightman, *Roman Trier and the Treveri* (London 1970), 145–48.

32. Collingwood, *Archaeology of Roman Britain*, 121–23.

33. E.M. Clifford, *Transactions of the Bristol and Gloucestershire Archaeological Society* 73 (1954), 5–69; cf. plan, *Britannia* 1 (1970), 294, fig. 9.

34. Wightman, *Roman Trier and the Treveri*, 142–43.

35. *Victoria County History Oxfordshire* 1 (1939), 316–18.

36. *Victoria County History Somerset* 1 (1906), 326–28.

37. R. Agache and B. Bréart, *Atlas d'archéologie aérienne de Picardie* (Amiens 1975); R. Agache, *La Somme pré-romaine et romaine* (Amiens 1978).

38. Agache, *La Somme pré-romaine et romaine*, 319, fig. 14.

39. *Victoria County History Sussex* 3 (1935), 20–23.

40. G. Fouet, *La villa gallo-romaine de Montmaurin (Hte.-Garonne)* (*Gallia* Suppl. 20, Paris, 1969).

41. J. Lauffray, J. Schreyek and N. Dupré, *Gallia* 31 (1973), 123–56.

42. Gorges, *Les villas hispano-romaines*, 267–68, with Pl. XLII.

43. John Hadman, 'Aisled buildings in Britain', in Todd (ed.), *Studies in the Romano-British Villa*, 187–95.

44. R. Goodburn, 'Winterton: some villa problems', in Todd (ed.) *Studies in the Romano-British Villa,* 93–101.

45. A. Moray Williams, *Archaeological Journal* 55 (1908), 57–60; 56 (1909), 33–52.

46. A.J. Evans, *Archaeological Journal* 54 (1897), 340–54.

47. D.J. Smith, 'The mosaic pavements', in Rivet (ed.), *The Roman Villa in Britain* 71–125.

48. John Percival, *The Roman Villa* (Batsford 1976), 174–76.

49. *Letters*, 2.2.

50. M. Blanchard-Lemée, 'La *villa* à mosaïques de Mienne-Marboué (Eure-et-Loir)', *Gallia* 39 (1981), 63–83.

51. *Gallia* 32 (1974), 480–81; 34 (1976), 487–89; 36 (1978), 415–18; 38 (1980), 491–92.

52. Collingwood, *Archaeology of Roman Britain*, 113.

4

Palaces

IAN M. BARTON

Later he lived on the Palatine, but still in a modest residence which had
belonged to [the orator] Hortensius, conspicuous neither for extent nor
for elegance: it contained only short colonnades of stone from the Alban
Hills, and the rooms had no marble decoration or figured pavements . . .
The simplicity of his household goods and furniture may still be seen
from surviving couches and tables, most of which scarcely attain the
refinement appropriate to a private citizen.

(Suetonius, *Augustus* 72–73)

The testimony of Suetonius, who in this part of his biography of
Augustus is concerned to produce evidence of the emperor's *continentia*
(moderation, restraint), has to be regarded with some scepticism in view
of excavations carried out in the south-west quarter of the Palatine hill
since 1956.[1] These have revealed the remains of a house built on two
levels, terraced on the slope of the hill. Adjacent is the massive podium
of a temple, with a gallery running towards the site of the libraries of the
later Palace of Domitian, which have the same orientation as the temple
and the house. The painted decoration of several of the rooms dates the
house to the 30s and 20s B.C., the early Augustan period, which is also
the date of the paintings in another house immediately north of it, which

has long been known as the 'House of Livia' (Augustus' wife); the identification is founded on the discovery there of water pipes stamped IVLIA AVGVSTA (the title by which she was known after her husband's death).

Comparison of the literary evidence for Augustus' house makes it virtually certain that this is the building in question. With slight divergences of detail, Velleius Paterculus (writing in A.D. 30), Suetonius and Dio agree on the following sequence of events.[2] On returning to Rome after his victory over Sextus Pompeius (36 B.C.), Caesar (as he was then called) began buying up properties adjacent to his own (i.e. the former residence of Hortensius) with a view to extending it. However, part of the site was struck by lightning, and consequently had to be consecrated to Apollo and declared public property. Thereupon he began the construction of the Temple of Apollo with adjacent porticoes and a pair of libraries (one Greek, one Latin), the whole complex being ready for dedication in 28 B.C.; while on the remainder of the site he built his own house, part of which was to be consecrated to Vesta after his election as *pontifex maximus* in 12 B.C.[3]

Here then we have the first official imperial residence on the Palatine hill. The preservation of its lower level is due to the fact that at some date subsequent to the Neronian fire of A.D. 64 it was filled in, probably to provide a foundation for an extension of Domitian's palace. Suetonius' account makes it clear that, although some at least of the furniture was preserved in his day, the house itself was no longer to be seen. The upper level, some 7–9 m above, incorporated (or perhaps replaced) a house of late Republican date (A on the plan, fig. 31); perhaps this was the original house of Hortensius, but there are also remains of similar buildings under the podium of the temple. The extant part of the house is clearly divided into three main sections: a range of rooms (7–11) symmetrically arranged, opening off a verandah along the north side of a peristyle, perhaps a garden; to the west a range of smaller rooms (1–6) opening off a corridor running north-south; while on the east side of the peristyle another range of rooms leads to a ramp which originally led up to the area in front of the entrance steps of the Temple of Apollo. There are also undecorated rooms behind 7–11 which lacked direct light and were presumably for service or storage. It seems a reasonable assumption that the west group of rooms, together with those on the upper floor, formed the private quarters of the emperor and his family, while the rooms around the peristyle were the official reception rooms, their public nature emphasised by the intimate connection with the Temple of

Apollo. The physical layout of the building confirms the statement of
Dio, referring to its repair after damage by fire in A.D. 3:

> After building his house, Augustus made it all public property, either
> because of the contribution [to the expenses of rebuilding] which had
> been made by the public or because, being *pontifex maximus*, he wished
> to live in a house at once private and open to all.[4]

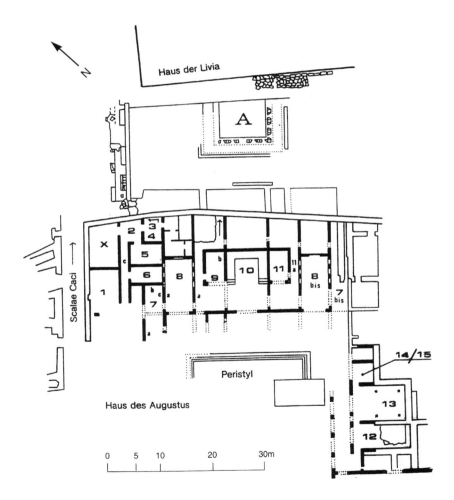

Fig. 31: Rome, Palatine: House of Augustus.

In line with the general ethos of the Augustan regime, Augustus was adapting to his new order the customs and practices of the Republican aristocracy. As we saw in Chapter 2, their houses served not only as private residences but also as the headquarters of their political ambitions, at which their *clientes* would gather for the formal morning reception (*salutatio*) before escorting the great man down to the Forum. What Augustus was doing, in effect, was to adapt his house to the needs of a situation in which the whole Roman people—senators and all—had become the *clientes* of one man, the *princeps*. Even before the end of the Augustan period, the word *Palatium* had begun to acquire the sense 'palace'—most strikingly in a passage where Ovid compares the 'kingly house of mighty Jove', surrounded by the stately houses of the 'divine nobility', to the Palatine, where Augustus' house was similarly situated among other sumptuous private houses.[5] Later the term was extended to cover imperial residences anywhere, as Dio, writing in the early third century, tells us:

> The imperial residence is called Palatium, not because there was ever a decree to this effect, but because Caesar [i.e. Augustus] lived on the Palatine and had his headquarters there . . . For this reason, even if the emperor is lodging somewhere else, his temporary residence keeps the title of Palatium.[6]

The next development in the evolution of the imperial property on the Palatine was the expansion of the Augustan complex by Gaius (37–41), who is said to have extended it as far as the Forum, turning the Temple of Castor into its vestibule; but there is no certain archaeological trace of this, nor of the bridge by which he is supposed to have joined it to the Capitol, unless the structures found in recent excavations behind the Temple of Castor are correctly interpreted as belonging to these developments.[7] (The 'Domus Tiberiana' in the north-west quarter of the Palatine was evidently a Neronian palace; no doubt it was so called because Tiberius' house had been among the earlier buildings it replaced, traces of which are detectable in the remains under the Farnese gardens.[8])

Perhaps it was this project of Gaius' which inspired Nero's idea of extending the palace complex all the way from the Palatine to the Esquiline (where the imperial properties included the pleasure-grounds (*horti*) which Maecenas had bequeathed to Augustus)—a distance of about a kilometre. This Domus Transitoria ('House of Passage') was largely destroyed in the great fire of 64, though parts of it have been discovered, notably a *nymphaeum* (fountain-court) beneath Domitian's

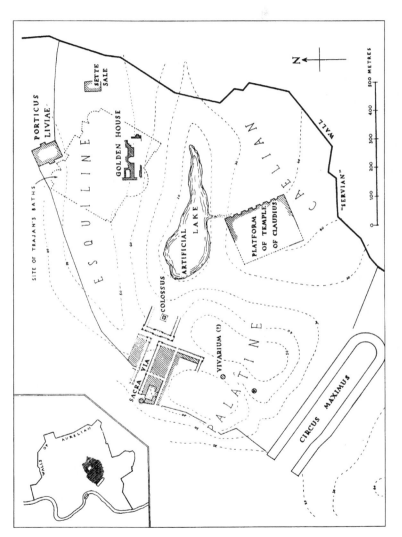

Fig. 32: Rome: general plan of Domus Aurea. Inset shows area occupied by Nero's estate compared with the city of Rome as enclosed by the Walls of Aurelian (late third century A.D.).

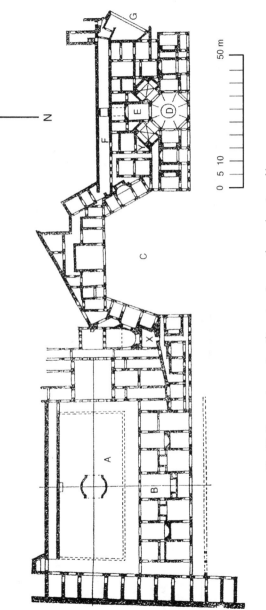

Fig. 33: Domus Aurea, Esquiline wing. See text for explanation of letters.

palace, and a rotunda spanning the intersection of two corridors at a point about midway between the two hills (beneath the podium of Hadrian's Temple of Venus and Rome). The fire gave Nero the opportunity to plan an even vaster new complex, the Domus Aurea ('Golden House'), which covered an area of some 50 ha (fig. 32). This ambitious scheme incorporated not only residential and reception wings but extensive parkland: Suetonius mentions a sea-like pond and 'countryside varied with fields, vineyards, pastures and woods, and great numbers of wild and domestic animals'.[9] Tacitus also describes 'fields and lakes and—giving an impression of uninhabited country—woods alternating with open spaces and views', and records the names of the architects Severus and Celer.[10] Clearly what Nero aimed at—improving on the tradition of *horti* like those of Maecenas—was a country villa in the heart of Rome; after his death (A.D. 68) the Flavian emperors who succeeded him threw it open as a public park.

The only substantial part of the Golden House to have survived is a wing on the southern slope of the Esquiline hill comprising nearly a hundred rooms along a frontage of some 200 m; it owes its preservation to its incorporation into the foundations of the Baths of Trajan (c. A.D. 104). The design of this wing shows a new freedom coming into Roman architecture, made possible by complete mastery of the structural use of concrete in the construction of walls, vaults and domes. How far the wing originally extended is unknown; if, as seems possible, the octagon (room D on fig. 33) was on the central axis of a symmetrical plan, wall G may mark the perimeter of another five-sided court corresponding with C, with further rooms beyond. The arrangement of rooms round the western courtyard (A) is not particularly unusual, though the subtle alternation of forms in hall B and its flanking rooms is worth notice. It is in the departure from rectangular forms around court C and the octagon that the true originality of the design appears, though it must be admitted that the architect has not been entirely successful in integrating these rooms into his overall plan; rooms X and Y, for example, are given an exceedingly awkward shape. Rabirius was to deal more cleverly with this problem twenty years later (see below, pp. 104f).

The most daring innovation is the octagonal hall with its dependencies: the photograph (pl. 15) and the plan (fig. 34) show how boldly the architect has here organised space. The central hall is in effect a ring of eight massive pillars supporting flat-arch lintels, thus creating a series of almost square openings, over each of which rises a segmental vault. As they rise, these vaults merge to form a flattish dome which is crowned

by a broad circular opening (*oculus*), 6 m in diameter.[11] Five of the
openings lead to a symmetrically arranged series of rooms, which are lit
from the gap between the outer surface of the dome and the top of the
octagonal wall fronting the rooms. The room (E) on the north-south axis
had a fountain in its inner niche, which was fed from cisterns higher up
the hill, the water being carried over the service corridor (F) by an arched
bridge. The whole suite may perhaps have been intended for summer
parties—the kind of occasion which led Nero to say that his new palace
let him 'at last begin to live like a human being'.[12]

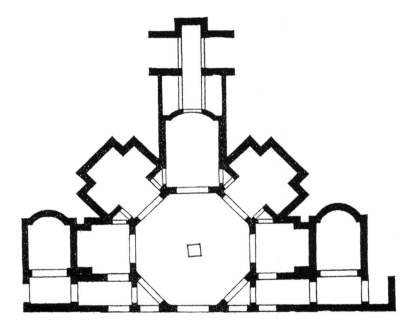

Fig. 34: Octagon room in Domus Aurea.

Before continuing with the development of the palace in Rome, it
may be as well to look at some imperial country residences, since, as has
been said, the Golden House is essentially in the tradition of luxurious
country houses. The island of Capreae (Capri), off the bay of Naples,
was bought by Augustus from the Neapolitans in 29 B.C.,[13] and seems
to have become a favourite holiday retreat; Suetonius recounts details of
a short holiday which Augustus spent there in August, A.D. 14, shortly

before his death.[14] Tacitus refers to twelve villas on the island in Tiberius' time,[15] though there are only three of which substantial remains are still to be seen. Of these the most impressive stands on the cliff-top (334 m above sea level) at the eastern end of the island, and is certainly to be identified as the emperor's principal residence, which

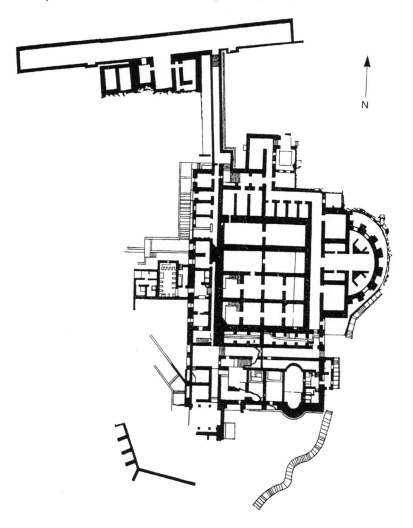

N

Fig. 35: Capri: Villa Iovis.

Pliny called *Tiberii principis arx* ('the emperor Tiberius' citadel'), and which is generally supposed to be the one Suetonius calls the Villa Iovis.[16] Here at the time of his coup against Sejanus (A.D. 31), Tiberius 'watched from the highest point of the cliff for the signals which he had ordered to be raised at a distance' (i.e. presumably on the mainland). The buildings (fig. 35) are arranged round a central square platform which covered a huge system of concrete barrel-vaulted cisterns, the storage of rainwater being the only practicable means of securing an adequate supply of water at such a height; their total capacity was around 12 million litres. The only entrance to the complex was by a vestibule at the south-west corner, leading to service rooms, including a large kitchen, in the west range, and a large suite of baths placed on the south side so as to catch the sun through large windows (cf. the Forum Baths at Ostia). Past the baths the corridor turned left into the official wing, the central feature of which was a large semicircular audience hall (*aula*) with smaller flanking rooms. Little of the superstructure of this wing now survives, and the plan is not entirely clear; the remaining walls are probably those of basement rooms, the main reception suite being on an upper level, with windows affording spectacular views over the sea. Beyond, the corridor again turned left and then right to reach the emperor's private quarters; none but the most privileged would be allowed to penetrate so far, and only a single narrow stairway connected it with the service wing. The tightness of security here makes a striking contrast with Augustus' ideal of a residence 'at once private and open to all'. From this wing the emperor could walk out into the gardens which probably occupied the upper terrace, or down to a loggia (*ambulatio*) facing north on the cliff edge, where a summer dining-room *(triclinium)*, with a vaulted ceiling and a floor paved with coloured marble, and adjacent rooms for rest or study (*cubicula*) provided a self-contained suite and area for exercise.

The other imperial villas on Capri include that now called Damecuta, at the west end of the island, which has a similar north-facing *ambulatio*[17] with, at one end, an apsidal belvedere comparable in size to the *aula* of the Villa Iovis, and, at the other, a suite of tiny rooms, approached down a steep flight of steps, which contained elegant works of art; surely again a private retreat for the emperor. There was also a seaside villa ('Palazzo a Mare') about halfway along the island's north coast, near the harbour; this was perhaps the original property of Augustus, but it was extensively damaged during the Napoleonic wars, and there is little record of its plan.

The imperial family certainly possessed country estates in other parts of Italy, just as the Republican nobility had done. Baiae, on the bay of Naples, was a favourite resort; the well-known story of Nero's murder of his mother Agrippina refers to *horti* at Tusculum and Antium as well as to two villas in the vicinity of Baiae.[18] Further north, on the coast near Terracina, Tiberius owned a villa built above a natural cavern, which was adapted by means of concrete walls and marble paving to serve as a banqueting hall and private theatre (cf. p. 148 and fig. 56). Excavation at the site, now called Sperlonga (a corruption of its ancient name *Spelunca*, 'the Grotto'), has recovered the remains of elaborate sculptural groups by Greek artists which adorned the grotto. It was here that Sejanus once saved Tiberius' life by sheltering him from a fall of rock with his own body. There was also a palatial villa at Sirmio (Sirmione) on Lake Garda in the north (pl. 16), though that may have belonged to an imperial favourite rather than to the emperor himself.[19] Perhaps it is something of an exaggeration to classify sites like these (Sandringhams rather than Windsors?) as palaces; yet Suetonius, in his account of the incident just mentioned, describes Spelunca as a *praetorium*, which seems to imply some kind of official status. It must be admitted, however, that by Suetonius' time the word could be used to mean any large mansion— a semantic development which itself is not without significance.[20]

One imperial country residence which was undoubtedly used for official purposes is that of Domitian near Alba—the *Albanum*. This estate, about 20 km from Rome on the Appian Way, and once the property of Pompey the Great, was acquired by Domitian during the reign of his father Vespasian (69–79). Here he laid out a vast complex on the hillside which slopes up to Lake Albano in its volcanic crater, reshaping it into three huge terraces. The buildings here included—as well as residential quarters for the emperor and his entourage— *nymphaea,* a theatre and baths; the combination of these with ornamental gardens and parkland recalls the planning of Nero's Golden House, though it was even more extensive. Credit for the design should probably be given to Rabirius, who is well attested as the architect of Domitian's palace in Rome (see below, pp. 102ff). Unfortunately few detailed investigations have been carried out there, and much remains uncertain; but the references in contemporary literature to this elegant and luxurious residence[21] suggest that this was where Domitian spent most of his time when not in Rome. Both Tacitus and Juvenal call it his *arx* (cf. Pliny's description of the Villa Iovis, p. 100 above).[22] For its use for official purposes, we have the evidence not only of the parody of an imperial privy council meeting in Juvenal's *Fourth Satire* but of an inscription of A.D. 82 in which the emperor publishes his judgement in a lawsuit after consultation with his advisers: the decree is dated 'in the Alban villa' (*in Albano*).[23] Albanum was not the only place to be used for such purposes; another inscription of A.D. 91 includes an imperial letter issued 'at Circeii' (*Circeiis*),[24] where he had a seaside villa which may have been almost as large. We are by this time (late first century A.D.) well on the way to the situation described by Dio (above, p. 94), where 'the Palace' is wherever the emperor happens to be residing.

The most impressive monument of Domitian's reign is the great palace in Rome which virtually completed the imperial take-over of the Palatine hill, occupying the whole of its eastern half, with a total area of rather over 3 ha, about twice that of the Domus Tiberiana. Here again we find the division into official and private sectors: the public reception rooms, usually referred to as the Domus Flavia, arranged round a vast peristyle court, occupy the western half of the site, adjoining the Domus Tiberiana; while the residential part, called the Domus Augustana,[25] covers a similar area, but with a southward extension on two levels. East of this again is a sunken garden surrounded by a two-storey colonnade.

In designing this huge complex (fig. 36), Domitian's architect Rabirius was concerned to juxtapose an immensely impressive series of public rooms with a private residence which, while furnishing accommodation for all the persons attendant on the emperor, would also provide their master with an elegant and luxurious retreat. The Domus Flavia was approached by a street leading up from the Arch of Titus in the Forum to an open space, the Area Palatina, which was overlooked by the north front of the platform on which the palace stands, forming here a colonnaded terrace (1 on fig. 36). Behind the colonnade were the three principal public rooms: in the centre a huge hall (3), about 32 m wide by 38 m long, which must have been the emperor's audience hall or throne room (it is usually referred to as the Aula Regia); on the left as you face the entrance is a smaller room (2), conventionally but without evidence called the Lararium (domestic chapel); on the right, an apsed basilica (4) about 20 m in width.

There is much controversy over the question of how these halls were roofed. A well-known conjectural restoration of the palace, first published in 1900 (pl. 17), shows the basilica with a timbered ceiling and flat roof and the 'Aula Regia' covered with a barrel vault. However, the fact that the outer side wall of the basilica was later provided with buttresses strongly suggests that it had a vaulted roof, whose thrust

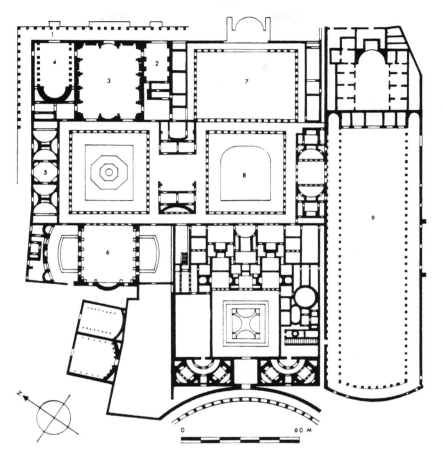

Fig. 36: Rome, Palatine: Domus Augustana (Domitian's Palace). General plan of upper level. 1. entrance colonnade of Domus Flavia; 2. 'Lararium'; 3. 'Aula Regia' (throne room?); 4. Basilica; 5. vestibule of (?) guest suite; 6. Triclinium; 7,8. peristyles of Domus Augustana; 9. 'Hippodrome' garden.

began to prove too much for the unsupported wall (the opposite wall was of course buttressed by the bulk of the adjacent hall). The 'Aula Regia' is more problematic. MacDonald[26] believes that it, like the hall ('vestibule') built at Forum level behind the Temple of Castor and the almost equally wide *triclinium* of the palace (see below), was barrel-vaulted, as shown in plate 17, and finds corroboration of this in the admiring descriptions of Statius (see below) and Martial ('this palace with its pinnacle touches the stars'; 'heaven with its stars ...').[27] Others, like Ward-Perkins and Sear,[28] doubt the possibility of raising a concrete vault over so wide a span. The greatest vaulted spans otherwise known in Roman architecture are all of around 25 m (e.g. Templum Pacis, Baths of Caracalla, Basilica of Maxentius); this distance, about 85 Roman feet, was perhaps regarded as the widest practicable span. If Rabirius had successfully spanned widths of 100 Roman feet (29.6 m) or more with vaults, one might have expected later architects to follow suit.

The same uncertainty attaches to the *triclinium* or banqueting hall (6) which formed the centre piece of the south wing, across the broad peristyle courtyard. It is flanked by two small patio-like enclosures with fountains in the middle; windows in the side walls provided views into these for the delectation of the diners. This is most likely to be the hall described in highly rhetorical terms by Statius, in a poem of thanks to the emperor for a banquet to which he had been unexpectedly invited. He speaks of 'the vast expanse of the pile, and the wide sweep of the hall, more open than a field, enclosing in its shelter a quantity of air', and goes on: 'Far above is the view; scarcely does the tired vision attain the summit; you would think it the golden ceiling of the sky'. This certainly seems to imply the presence of a roof of some kind, but the description is far too imprecise to give any clear indication. At least we can picture Domitian on the dais at the south end (pl. 18), presiding over 'the leaders of Rome [i.e. senators] and the troops of *equites*, reclining at a thousand tables at once'.[29] As a matter of sober fact, the maximum capacity of the hall, if the diners were reclining in the normal Roman fashion, would have been about 600 guests.

The peristyle courtyard of the Domus Flavia was laid out as a garden, with a large octagonal basin in the centre. The side ranges contained rooms of varied shapes, including an octagon in the centre of the west wing (5). Although on a slightly smaller scale than the rooms in the Domus Aurea,[30] they are more cleverly planned, with doorways providing interesting glimpses from each room into its neighbours; there are none of the awkwardly shaped remnants and wasted spaces that we noted in the octagon wing of the Domus Aurea. A broad passageway through the east range leads into the identically sized central piazza of the Domus Augustana, the central feature of which was a sunken pool (8) with an island in the middle. This also stands on the longitudinal axis of this half of the palace, which led from an entrance portico of which little remains, across a broad peristyle entrance court (7), and then through the piazza to the upper level of the residential wing.

This wing has been well described by MacDonald as 'an extra-ordinary mosaic of chambers of rectilinear and curving plan . . . They were not carried to an even level but were given various heights in order to light their interiors. Here Rabirius utterly abandoned the vocabulary of the past. He led the visitor through bewildering chains of spaces that now expanded, then contracted.'[31] The same elaborate connection from room to room is seen here as in the west wing of the Domus Flavia; in neither was it possible to walk from end to end in a straight line along the longitudinal axis, but here, with the larger number of rooms involved, the effect was even more intricate.

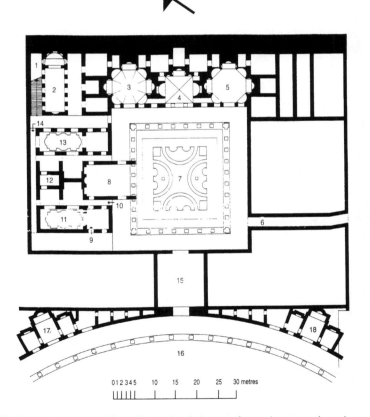

Fig. 37: Domus Augustana. Plan of lower level. See text for explanation of numbers.

The rooms continued round all four sides of the light well above the garden court of the lower level, though little now remains of any rooms except those of the north range. On the south side a pair of summer houses (*diaetae*) backed on to the upper level of a broad exedra overlooking the Circus Maximus. The only approach to the lower level is by a narrow staircase at the north-west corner, though there seems once to have been another on the east side. Domitian, like Tiberius, was obsessed with security;[32] what was probably the emperor's private suite is a self-contained group of rooms, all interconnected, on the west side of the garden on the lower level (8–13 on fig. 37). But the most interesting rooms in this part of the palace are the suite on the north side, where octagonal rooms (3, 5) flank a central square chamber (4). The octagons, of similar size to that in the Domus Aurea, have alternating rectangular and semicircular recesses which reduce their walls to eight brick-faced pillars supporting the domical vault; the square room, again with virtually no solid walls, was probably roofed with a groined cross-vault.

Domitian's palace was completed by (*a*) the sunken walled garden in the shape of a hippodrome (9 on fig. 36; the conceit extends to the provision of *carceres* at its north end), which was entered by a narrow passageway from the east side of the private garden (6 on fig. 37); (*b*) the curved facade on the south side overlooking the Circus Maximus; and (*c*) the libraries already mentioned, on the site of those founded by Augustus (above, p. 91). Although further structures were added under Hadrian (117–138) and Septimius Severus (193–211) to both this and the Domus Tiberiana, they made no essential change to the basic layout of the palace. The most spectacular of these additions was the *Septizodium*, a huge screen resembling the *scaenae frons* of a Roman theatre, which stood at the south corner of the Severan extension, intended, so it was said,[33] to impress visitors from Africa (Septimius' home province) arriving in Rome along the Appian Way with the magnificence of their fellow-countryman's imperial residence.

If the Domus Augustana marks the culmination of the development of the palace in the capital, the most magnificent of the imperial country properties is the great complex built by Hadrian between 118 and 138 below the town of Tibur (Tivoli). It is now generally known as Hadrian's Villa (Villa Adriana); but 'villa' is really too modest a description of this vast site, the excavated remains of which cover an area of over 30 ha, and which is estimated, on the evidence of other remains found in the vicinity, to have occupied originally between five and ten times this area.

At least one country house of the late Republican period stood on the site; some of its walls were incorporated into rooms around the 'Palace Peristyle' (17 on fig. 38). The plan of the site is not easy to understand; we cannot even be certain that the surviving remains are the main part of the palace. However, the buildings are not simply disposed casually; there does seem to be evidence of planning of individual sections around five main axes (marked A–E on fig. 39). It is doubtful whether any of the extant structures can be identified with the souvenirs of his travels which Hadrian is said to have incorporated into the palace;[34] perhaps the most probable of the traditional applications of names is that of Canopus (a canal linking Alexandria with the Nile) to the long narrow lake (12 on fig. 38) flanked by works of art (pl. 19) and leading to a great semi-circular *nymphaeum*, which may have been intended to recall the famous Serapeum of Alexandria. A detailed description of the buildings cannot be attempted here; it will be sufficient to draw attention to some of the most interesting features.

One of the most striking characteristics is the extensive use made of water, which recalls the lakes of Nero's Golden House (above, p. 97). As well as the 'Canopus' just mentioned, there is the large rectangular basin (fishpond or swimming-pool?) which occupies the centre of the huge piazza (7) on axis A, which is traditionally but certainly wrongly labelled 'Poecile' (nothing could be less like the Painted Stoa in Athens!); and smaller ponds and fountains adorn many of the buildings. Just to the south-east of the 'Poecile' is a garden laid out in the shape of a stadium (9), like the 'hippodrome' of the Domus Augustana, though it is somewhat smaller (c.125 m long as against c.150 m).[35] At its southern end is a semicircular *exedra* which contained an ornamental fountain (*nymphaeum*), and there was at least one pool among the flower-beds north of the central cross-axis. This axis joins a large dining-room (8), which has semicircular *exedras* on three sides and a rectangular pool on the north (where it adjoins the 'Poecile'), with a group of rooms leading, on a higher level, to a rectangular courtyard in which a colonnade surrounds another large pool, perhaps intended as a swimming-pool. Beneath this colonnade is one of the many *cryptoporticus* (enclosed corridors) which are a notable feature of the palace, providing sub-terranean connections between its various sections.

The gem of the whole palace is the round building traditionally misnamed the 'Maritime Theatre'; a better name would be 'Island Pavilion' (4). In the plan of the complex, it acts as a pivot between the two main alignments A (Poecile–Stadium) and C (Great Peristyles), and

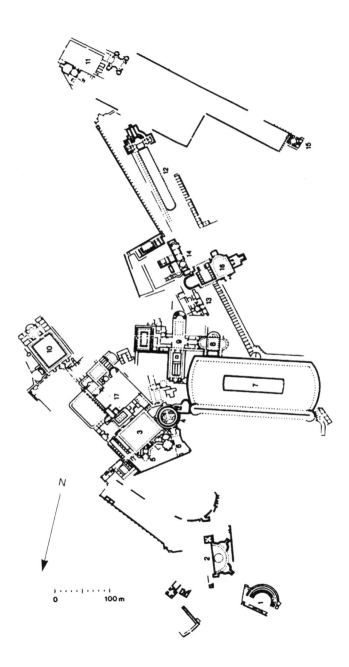

Fig. 38: Hadrian's Villa: general plan. 1. 'Greek theatre'; 2. 'Temple of Aphrodite (Venus Cnidia)' (cf. plate 22); 3. 'Libraries' terrace; 4. island pavilion ('Maritime Theatre'); 5,6. 'Libraries' (cf. fig. 50); 7. 'Poecile'; 8. summer dining room (*triconchos*); 9. 'Stadium' garden (cf. fig. 51); 10. 'Piazza d'Oro': 11. 'Academy'; 12. 'Canopus', with 'Serapeum' at south end (cf. fig. 55); 13. small baths; 14. large baths; 15. tower; 16. vestibule (?main entrance of palace); 17. site of Republican villa.

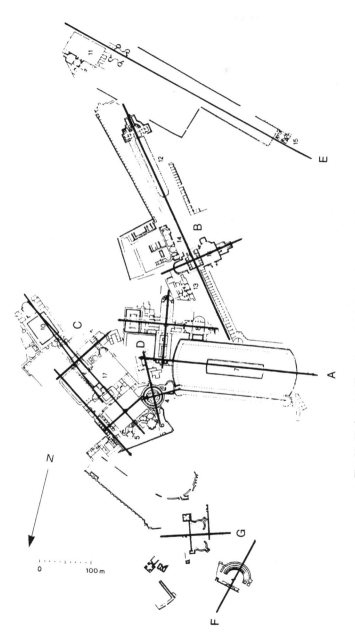

Fig. 39: Hadrian's Villa: schematic plan, showing axes of planning.

gives access to a private bath suite on an intermediate alignment (D). The core of this building is a miniature villa of circular plan (diameter about 25 m), consisting of three suites of small rooms surrounding a garden courtyard, itself approached through a semicircular vestibule. The villa is surrounded by a shallow canal 4.8 m wide, which in turn is surrounded by a colonnade of forty unfluted Ionic columns (pl. 20). It could only be crossed by a drawbridge, so that when this was raised the place was completely isolated; this must surely have been, in the tradition of such places noted earlier, the emperor's private retreat.

Just as the Domus Augustana is the climax of the Palatine buildings in Rome, so Hadrian's pleasure grounds at Tibur mark the culmination of the development of the imperial properties outside the capital, though, like the Julio-Claudian and Flavian emperors, Hadrian and his successors possessed, and used, estates elsewhere in Italy. He himself died at Baiae, while his successor Antoninus Pius (138–161) built a 'palace' at Lorium, about 16 km west of Rome, which had been his boyhood home, and where he died.[36] In one of his letters, the younger Pliny gives an account of court life at an imperial residence—Trajan's 'villa' at Centumcellae (Civitavecchia; possibly the complex to which belonged the bath suite whose ruins are now known as Terme Taurine):

> Our days were taken up with serious matters, but we enjoyed our relaxations in the evenings. The Emperor invited us to dinner every day, a simple affair if you consider his position. Sometimes we were entertained by recitations, or else the night was prolonged by pleasant conversation, and, on our last day, with his usual thoughtful generosity, he sent us all parting gifts. I took great pleasure in . . . the charm and informality of our social life, and I was no less delighted in the place itself.[37]

Besides the imperial residences in Rome and Italy, there are building complexes in the provinces to which the designation 'palace' may justifiably be applied. Official residences provided for provincial governors and army commanders come into this category, particularly as they may well have served for the accommodation of an emperor on his tours of the Empire (Hadrian, of course, is the outstanding example, cf. below, p. 113); on such occasions, they would become temporary *palatia* in accordance with Dio's definition (above, p. 94). But we may also use the word to describe residences of client kings (in Latin, properly *regiae*).

The most striking example is certainly the palace which Herod the Great built for himself on the barren rock of Masada in the Judaean desert, involving as it did engineering works of immense complexity. Here, as in the Villa Iovis on Capri (above, p. 100), an elaborate system of security gave the ruler a private retreat inaccessible to unauthorised persons; in this instance the official reception areas, including a throne room, were contained in a separate building on the west side of the rock. The whole of the top was occupied by an array of storehouses, and cut into the rock were several large cisterns—essential in that waterless area. At the north end the king's private residence was arranged on three terraces, of which the uppermost has a house of relatively modest dimensions, while the lowest, some 33 m below, is enlarged by a huge artificial platform to carry a secluded belvedere commanding a view of the valley below.

In complete contrast, at the other end of the Empire, is the palatial villa at Fishbourne near Chichester which is thought to have been provided for the British client king Cogidubnus (c. A.D. 75). The main palace occupied some 2 ha, and, taking into account the evidence for outlying buildings and for a terraced garden running down to the sea on the southern side, the entire villa must have occupied at least 5 ha. Its official character appears in several ways: (a) it is much larger than any contemporary villa in Britain, larger even than most of the great fourth-century villas;[38] (b) its formal plan, with four large wings ranged round a spacious central garden, is reminiscent of the Domus Tiberiana; (c) the palace was approached through an impressive entrance hall, directly opposite which is the central room of the west wing, which had an apsidal recess in its west wall, showing that it was designed as a throne room or audience chamber; and (d) at the north-east corner of the complex an aisled building, which could only be entered from outside, seems to have been designed as an assembly hall for semi-public functions.

Apart from the slight irregularity of the east wing, which was caused by the incorporation of an earlier building of Neronian date (the excavators called it the 'proto-palace'), the plan of the complex is strikingly regular; perhaps military engineers were employed on the project. Similar plans (though on a smaller scale) may be seen in the legates' residences of legionary fortresses (cf. Chapter 6 below), and in the palaces that were provided for army commanders and provincial governors. A striking example of such a structure, apparently intended for temporary use during a particular operation, has recently been uncovered at the British frontier site of Vindolanda (Chesterholm, just south of Hadrian's Wall). Here the fifth period of occupation, which can

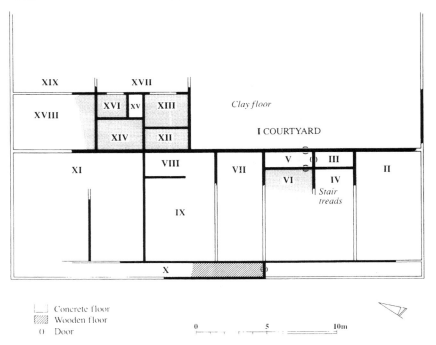

Fig. 40: Vindolanda: Hadrianic 'palace'.

be dated c.120–130, included a large timber-framed building of at least two wings arranged round a courtyard (fig. 40). Constraints on excavation beneath the preserved structures of the later fort mean that the full plan will never be recoverable; but if, as seems probable, it was more or less symmetrical, the whole building would have been about 29 m square, and contained at least forty rooms on the ground floor. The discovery of stair treads in the debris above room IV shows that at least that end of the west wing had an upper storey. The framework of the building consisted of massive oak sleeper beams (one left behind by the demolition squad was 5.4 m long and 32 x 28 cm in section) to which uprights were bolted at an average interval of 4.8 m; these were so deeply embedded in the ground that the demolishers had simply sawn them off at ground level. The walls were of wattle, rendered with plaster. Rooms VI, VII and VIII had painted wall plaster; room VI and several of the rooms in the north wing had floors of *opus signinum*. The roof was of oak shingles. That so relatively elaborate a temporary structure (it

appears to have remained in use for no longer than ten years) should
have been erected at what was, after all, only an auxiliary fort site has
been thought to suggest the possibility that it was directly connected
with the building of Hadrian's Wall, which began at the time of the
emperor's visit to the army in Britain in 120. With due caution, therefore, it may be surmised that this was Hadrian's own headquarters
during his stay on the northern frontier.[39]

As the frontier system of the Empire became more permanent, much
larger stone residences were constructed for officials in the provinces,
like the partially excavated second-century palace of the governor of
Lower Pannonia at Aquincum (Budapest) and the third-century palace of
the *dux ripae* at Dura-Europus on the Euphrates, both of which show
arrangements of rooms round one or more peristyle courtyards. In some
cases at least these residences (like perhaps the temporary structure at
Vindolanda) provided accommodation for emperors and their suites,
and thus became *palatia* in the full sense. A well-known example is the
palace of the governor of Upper Pannonia at Carnuntum (Petronell in
Lower Austria), which served as the headquarters of Marcus Aurelius
while he was personally directing operations on the Danube frontier
during the Marcomannic War of 171–173. The area enclosed by its
perimeter wall is still not as great as that of the Fishbourne palace (about
1.5 ha), but excavation has revealed a group of rooms arranged round a
great hall with an apsed recess at one end. This block, with its system of
central heating, may conceivably have been built to provide suitable
accommodation for the ceremonial and judicial functions which the
emperor was expected to perform. As Sir Ian Richmond put it,
'*Carnuntum* provides, as no other site in the Empire yet does, an idea of
what sort of building might be erected for an Imperial residence when
the Emperor planned a prolonged stay in a province'.[40]

The best preserved of all Roman palaces is the one which Diocletian
built (c.300) for his retirement on the Dalmatian coast near his birth-
place Salonae (Solin). It is virtually a walled fortress, approximately 200
x 160 m, divided into four quarters by broad colonnaded streets crossing
at the centre (fig. 41). In the Middle Ages the town of Split grew up
within its walls, ensuring its preservation almost intact, and it seems to
have remained relatively unscathed by recent events in Croatia. The two
northern sectors appear to have contained barracks; there would have
been accommodation for between 500 and 600 soldiers. On the seaward
side of the main east–west street, which corresponds to the *uia praetoria*
of a military camp, the north–south street (*uia principalis*) becomes an

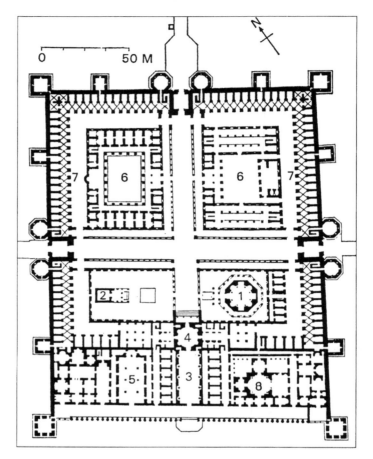

Fig. 41: Split: Diocletian's palace. 1. emperor's mausoleum; 2. temple; 3. great hall; 4. domed vestibule; 5. audience chamber; 6. residential blocks; 7. barracks; 8. banqueting suite.

arcaded court, called the 'Peristyle' (pl. 21), which is flanked on the west by a temple precinct (2 on fig. 41) and on the east by the emperor's mausoleum (1); in death, as in life, an emperor no longer needed to be based in Rome. At the end of the 'Peristyle', a domed circular vestibule (4) leads to a large rectangular entrance hall (3), the central feature of the official suite, which included to the west a basilical audience chamber (5) comparable in size to the Basilica of the Domus Flavia, and to the east a square room with apsidal recesses (8) which is reminiscent of the similarly sized octagonal rooms in Nero's and Domitian's palaces; presumably, like them, it was roofed with a dome. Several smaller rooms open off it; the whole group should probably be regarded as a suite for formal banqueting. All these rooms are linked by a gallery running the entire length of the south side, with an arcade overlooking the sea; at either end are the emperor's private quarters, including a bath suite.

The division of the Empire into four parts, and the increasingly peripatetic lifestyle of the emperors, necessitated the building of several new imperial residences. The arrangements at Split, especially the 'Peristyle' and the arcaded gallery, have a marked similarity to the description by Libanius (writing in 356 or 360) of the palace at Antioch which Diocletian had constructed before 298:

> Three of these [colonnaded streets in the 'new city' on an island in the river Orontes], running as far as the wall, are joined to the perimeter, but the fourth is shorter, but more beautiful in proportion to its shortness, since it acts as an entrance [*propylaea*] to the palace, which begins nearby. The palace itself occupies as much as a quarter of the whole island. It reaches to the middle . . . and extends to the outer branch of the river, so that where the wall has columns in place of battlements a view worthy of an emperor is afforded, of the river flowing below and the suburbs delighting the eye in all directions.[41]

The contrast of these self-contained units with the open plan of Nero's, Domitian's and Hadrian's palaces is a reflexion of the increasing militarisation of the Empire; nothing could be less like the Augustan ideal of a *domus* 'open to all'. Yet even in the fourth century other imperial residences seem to have retained a predominantly civilian character, like the palaces of the Caesars Galerius (293–311) at Thessalonike (Salonika) and Constantius (293–306) at Augusta Treverorum (Trier), both of which were integrated into the town plans, of which they took up a considerable part. At Trier the 'basilica'—twice the size of the 'throne room' at Split—and a surviving part of the imperial baths attest the splendour of Constantius' capital.

The most impressive country house of the late Empire, the villa at Piazza Armerina in central Sicily, has also been claimed as an imperial residence. It is not the only conspicuously luxurious house of the period—several villas, including that at Montmaurin (p. 83), are comparable in size—but it is distinguished both by the unorthodox complexity of its plan and by the exceptional quantity and quality of its mosaic decoration; practically every room is adorned with figured

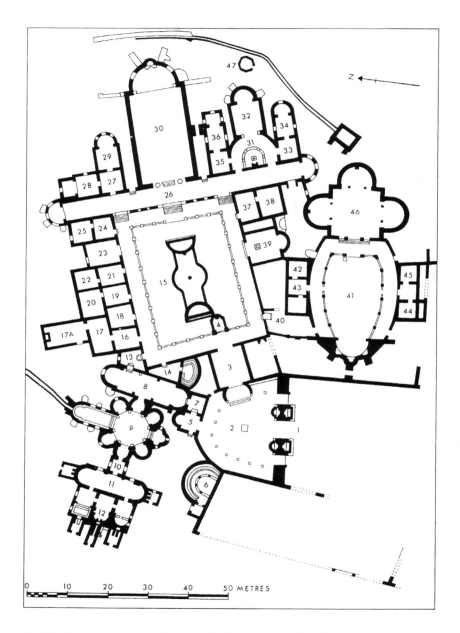

Fig. 42: Piazza Armerina: late-Imperial villa. See text for explanation of numbers.

mosaic floors, covering, it has been estimated, a total of c.3,500m².[42]
Although the archaeological evidence is uncertain, it seems to have been
built in the first quarter of the fourth century, on the site of a large
second-century villa which was demolished to make way for its successor. The excavated remains (fig. 42), comprising the 'palace' proper,
cover an area of some 1.5 ha, but the property must originally have been
considerably more extensive, with dependent buildings (servants'
quarters, store rooms etc.) beyond the excavated area.

The layout is in some respects reminiscent of Hadrian's Villa at
Tivoli, particularly in the combination of buildings on several different
axes. The main buildings are entered through a triple gateway (1), which
leads to an asymmetrical entrance courtyard (2), from which there was
access either directly to the bath suite (5–12) or through a vestibule (3)
to the great peristyle courtyard with a central ornamental pool (15),
around which the main living quarters are arranged. At the inner end of
the peristyle, steps lead up to a transverse corridor (26), 70 m long, the
whole floor of which is taken up by the huge mosaic composition known
as the 'Great Hunt', which shows exotic animals being captured and
transported by ship, presumably to Rome. The rooms opening off this
corridor on the east include a great apsed hall (30), with a small suite of
rooms (27–29) to the north, and a larger suite (31–36) to the south,
which is probably to be identified as the private living quarters of the
owner's family. These rooms are arranged round a semicircular court
with a fountain (31), and each of them is floored with mosaics, several
of which depict children playing. Finally, there is a separate group of
rooms to the south of the peristyle, the purpose of which is somewhat
enigmatic. A vast oval porticoed court (41), flanked by several small
rooms (42–45), leads to a three-apsed hall (triconchos, 46) with
elaborate mosaics celebrating the exploits of Hercules. The style of these
is so different from those in the rest of the villa that some scholars have
supposed this southern group to be a later addition, and this view might
be supported by the curiously obscure access routes to it: through room
40 from the peristyle, and by an oddly shaped passage leading from the
south end of the 'Great Hunt' corridor. However, the mosaics in rooms
42–45 are stylistically identical with others elsewhere in the villa, and
since they clearly belong to an arrangement designed to culminate in the
triconchos it seems better to suppose that the whole complex was built
at one time. This would not, of course, preclude the possibility that the
inclusion of the triconchos suite was a modification decided on during
building.

Was this villa, like Hadrian's, an imperial residence? Following a suggestion originally made by H.P. L'Orange in 1952,[43] several scholars have accepted the theory that we have here a counterpart to Diocletian's palace at Split, built for the retirement of his colleague Maximian. Others think it more likely to have belonged to his son Maxentius (emperor 306–312).[44] Either of these would be consistent with the archaeological evidence, though that would equally support a date in the reign of Constantine (312–337); and the Hercules symbolism of the *triconchos* would be appropriate to the dynasty of Maximian, who took Hercules as his patron. On the other hand, these emperors are not known to have had any connection with Sicily, and in fact Maximian, unlike his senior colleague, did not remain in retirement. Features of the Piazza Armerina villa can be paralleled in other houses of the period which there is no reason to associate with emperors (e.g. a *triconchos* at Patti Marina in north Sicily; another at Desenzano in north Italy, where the mosaics are almost as abundant and elaborate as at Piazza Armerina; large apsed halls at Milreu in Portugal, which may have been the most extensive of all, and at Löffelbach in Austria).[45] In the present state of our knowledge, it is probably safer to attribute Piazza Armerina to a wealthy aristocrat, probably—as the subject-matter of the 'Great Hunt' mosaic suggests—one who had made his fortune out of importing wild beasts for the shows in the amphitheatre at Rome. But the mere fact that this villa could be thought of as a possible imperial palace is an indication that, in the later years of the Empire as at its beginning, the essential difference between the residences of emperors and of the senatorial aristocracy was one of function rather than of scale and splendour.

NOTES

1. G. Carettoni, *Das Haus des Augustus auf dem Palatin* (Mainz 1983), deals mainly with the painted decoration. For a more general account of the site, see his article in *Rendiconti della Pontificia Academia di Archeologia* 39 (1966–7), 55–75.

2. Velleius Paterculus 2.81.3; Suetonius, *Augustus* 29.3; Dio 49.15.5; 53.1.3.

3. Ovid, *Fasti* 4.949–54.

4. Dio 55.12.5.

5. Ovid, *Metamorphoses* 1.168–76.

6. Dio 53.16.5f.

7. Suetonius, *Caligula* 22.2 & 4. Preliminary publication of the excavation by H. Hurst in *Archeologia laziale* 9 (1988), 16–17, in which he suggests that these structures were indeed the vestibule of Caligula's palace. He now has doubts about the interpretation, but hopes to settle these before the final publication (personal information from Mr Hurst). For the Augustan complex in general, see T.P. Wiseman, *Historiography and Imagination* (Exeter 1994), 102–11; *Death of an Emperor* (Exeter 1991), 104–10.

8. R. Locher and B. Sigel (eds), *Domus Tiberiana: nuove ricerche, studi di restauro* (Rome/Zurich 1985).

9. Suetonius, *Nero* 31.

10. Tacitus, *Annals* 15.42.

11. For comparison, the *oculus* of the Pantheon has a diameter of 8.3 m, but the diameter of its dome is nearly three times as great.

12. Suetonius, *Nero* 31.

13. Dio 52.43.

14. Suetonius, *Augustus* 98.

15. Tacitus, *Annals* 4.67.

16. Pliny, *Natural History* 3.82; Suetonius, *Tiberius* 65.

17. The compass point indicated by A.G. Mackay, *Houses, Villas and Palaces in the Roman World* (London 1975), fig. 44 (p. 117), is incorrect.

18. Tacitus, *Annals* 14.3.1 (Tusculum and Antium); 4.3 (Bauli, between Baiae and Misenum); 4.6 (Baiae itself); Suetonius, *Nero* 34.

19. Sperlonga: Tacitus, *Annals* 4.59; Suetonius, *Tiberius* 39. Sirmione: see T.P. Wiseman, *Roman Studies* (Liverpool 1987), 307–70; the place was in the territory of Verona, the home town of the poet Catullus, who himself had had a villa there (Catullus 31), and Valerii Catulli were close friends of Gaius (Suetonius, *Caligula* 36.1) and Domitian (Pliny, *Letters* 4.22.5).

20. Suetonius uses the word of imperial residences also at *Augustus* 72.3 (Augustus' granddaughter Julia); *Caligula* 37.2 (Caligula). But it can also denote properties of other citizens: e.g. Martial 10.79.1; Juvenal 1.75 (associated with *horti*).

21. E.g. Statius, *Silvae* 3.5.28; Suetonius, *Domitian* 19.

22. Tacitus, *Agricola* 45.1; Juvenal 4.145. Dio (67.1.2) calls it 'a kind of acropolis'.

23. M. McCrum & A.G. Woodhead, *Select documents of the principates of the Flavian emperors* (Cambridge 1961), 462, line 28.

24. The *lex Irnitana*, tablet XC, line 39: *Journal of Roman Studies* 76 (1986), 181 (text); 199 (translation).

25. In fact the official name of the whole palace seems to have been Domus Augustana (or Augustiana); but the distinction, even if a modern convention, is a convenient one.

26. MacDonald, *Architecture of the Roman Empire I* (New Haven 1982), 56–63.

27. Martial 8.36; 7.56.

28. Ward-Perkins, *Roman Imperial Architecture* (Harmondsworth 1981), 80; F. Sear, *Roman Architecture* (London 1982), 151.

29. Statius, *Silvae* 4.2.23–25; 30–31; 32–33. Statius himself was presumably of equestrian rank.

30. The diameter of the octagon room is approximately 12 m, compared with 13.5 m for the octagon room of the Domus Aurea.

31. MacDonald, *Architecture of the Roman Empire I*, 64.

32. For examples, see Suetonius, *Domitian* 14.

33. *Historia Augusta, Severus* 24.

34. *Historia Augusta, Hadrian* 26.5 mentions a Lyceum, Academy, Prytaneum, Canopus, Poecile, Tempe, and even an underworld. The tradition goes back at least to the late Republic: Cicero had an Academy and a Lyceum in his villa at Tusculum (Cicero, *Tusculan Disputations* 2.9); Atticus was collecting statues for the former between 68 and 66 B.C. (id. *ad Atticum* 1.6.2; 9.2; 11.3; 4.3).

35. For this, and further discussion of the gardens of Hadrian's Villa, see below, Chapter 5, pp. 138ff.

36. *Historia Augusta, Hadrian* 25.6; *Antoninus Pius* 1.8; 12.6. The site of the villa at Lorium has not been identified. The Antonine emperors also had a villa at Alsium, a little further along the Via Aurelia.

37. Pliny, *Letters* 6.31 (tr. B. Radice).

38. 'Even . . . the villa at Woodchester . . . could have been fitted,courtyards and all, into the formal garden' (B.W. Cunliffe, *Fishbourne; a Roman Palace and its Garden* [London 1971], 165). Cunliffe's account of the excavations (1961–69) should be consulted for full details.

39. Information about the 1992 and 1993 excavations at Vindolanda by personal communication from Mr Robin Birley.

40. I.A. Richmond, *Roman Archaeology and Art*, ed. P. Salway (London 1969), 265: from the text of a lecture on 'Roman provincial palaces'.

41. Libanius, *Oration* 11.205–6.

42. R.J.A. Wilson, *Piazza Armerina* (Austin 1983), 15. This book should be consulted for further details about the villa and its mosaics.

43. Most conveniently to be found in his collection *Likeness and Icon* (Odense 1973) in the paper 'Nouvelle contribution à l'étude de Palais Herculien de Piazza Armerina', pp. 196–205.

44. For references and a more detailed discussion, see Wilson, *Piazza Armerina*, 86ff.

45. Ibid., 75–85, for these and other parallels; for plans, see his figs 48, 50, 51.

5

The Roman Garden as a Domestic Building

Nicholas Purcell

I. Romulus and the Roman birthright

One of the ways in which people see themselves is as the practitioners of some particular form of agricultural production. In the Mediterranean, where the environment is very varied, it has perhaps usually been normal for human societies to practise diverse and mixed forms of production; but that has not prevented the pastoral or the arable, the cultivation of the grape, the olive or a cereal, from becoming the identifying mark of a cultural group.

One of the options available where labour is sufficient, the soil is rich, and above all where water is readily available, especially in the long Mediterranean summer drought, is the highly intensive cultivation of specialised plant crops or the rearing of animals that require considerable care. In many parts of the Mediterranean production is essentially twofold: intensive cultivation and management of the resources of the wild, establishing a balanced contrast between intensive cultivation and the wilderness, undisturbed by the existence of other forms of cultivation in between. Locally this sort of use of the environment is very often made on a small scale in a defined and confined place ('like a flower hidden away in fenced gardens, unknown to the herd, uprooted by no plough'[1]), and especially—but not exclusively—where plants are cared for in this way, this is what we would normally call intensive horticulture, and the place where it happens a garden.

The Romans thought that their early forebears, settled in Romulus' new city, had practised this sort of husbandry on the little lots that were the share of the environment apportioned to each citizen, and his stake in the land of the community. The Tiber offered water in abundance all year round, and the rainfall of the region of Rome is high enough to make garden cultivation possible, especially assisted by the water distribution skills at which the Romans early came to excel. A Roman in Romulus' day was thus by definition the owner of a *hortus*, and the plot of land in question was thought of as being in the closest relationship to the abode that was the other token of his belonging—as was natural, since the labour demands of horticulture usually preclude a productive garden's being located far from the homes of those who tend it. Deep in what the Romans thought about themselves, therefore, we find intensive horticulture and the lots on which it took place; and its domestic nature is central.[2]

II. Lots in country and town

Until the later Empire, the notion of a kind of citizen egalitarianism reflected in the size of lot enjoyed by each household in town or country remained an ingredient in Roman social and political thinking, sometimes an important one. The shares of public land allotted to soldiers in the Republic were often so small as to suggest that production at something like garden intensity was envisaged. Certainly the Romans felt that their forebears had subsisted to a large extent on vegetables. But the veteran's lot in the territory of a new town was mirrored in his share of the space of the town itself on which the settler was to build a house, and this too was very often partly given over to horticulture.

The division of land into a chequerboard of regular units made possible the equal sharing of the territory, and the Roman town too was divided evenly into blocks with roughly similar sized houses and patches of garden ground. The example of Pompeii shows this well. Within the walls a considerable amount of space always remained free from buildings and was intensively cultivated in small garden units for the production of all kinds of crop for the market. This urban landscape of gardens was given its character by the underlying principle of citizen householding which fragmented the townscape into hundreds of properties, many of which were still large enough to offer a productive opportunity to the proprietor. Not that much space was required; window-box production of vegetables was well worth while. We hear of exotics like cassia grown in this way, and the Elder Pliny, in a vein that is all too familiar, laments the days when Rome presented a much more verdant appearance:

> It was not so long ago either that the populace of the city of Rome used to provide in the windows a day-to-day experience of the countryside, a real spectacle of market gardens. Now the extraordinary increase in the number of violent burglaries has compelled everyone to shut off their outside views.³

In turn, the gardens also became an amenity: the pleasure of sitting in an arbour or dining *al fresco* in an urban vineyard or market garden was one which on the evidence of Pompeii had a considerable social diffusion, being shared by customers of wineshops as well as by the owners of larger houses (fig. 43). As an amenity, the garden was one of the things that could be made available to the community through the generosity of the benefactor—either opening a pleasance that was usually private, or making in perpetuity a place of resort, with trees and water, and buildings for refreshment or decoration, for the community to share. Such places do not seem to have been totally separate from the tradition of the private market garden and the commercial extension of it; they still often involved productive plantings rather than being somehow in a category of the 'wholly ornamental'.⁴ They are none-theless good examples of the attraction that the Romans called *amoenitas*, a complex mix of visual and conceptual ideas about the right landscape setting for the life of cultured leisure.

Another reflection of the allotted world of the Roman citizen parallels both the house-terrain of the town and the productive lot of the countryside: the garden-tomb.⁵ In death as in life Romans had their measured space—so many feet along the front, so many into the field, the dimensions on thousands of tombstones describe the plots housing the ashes of the dead which lined the roads outside the gates of Roman cities. Such places were not deserted cemeteries; they were the scene of the rites which commemorated the deceased, and were often laid out to accommodate the shared meals which formed part of those rites. So, just like the urban gardens, they often contained arbours and trees for shade, and the land was too valuable not to use for production; so tombs came to be set in sometimes lavish and elaborate lots, whose facilities are described with jealous precision on the tomb-inscriptions:

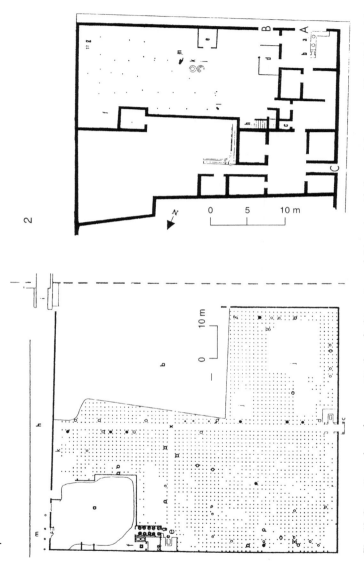

Fig. 43: Pompeii: gardens of taverns: (1) plan of a large vineyard. Note the grid-plan, and the tavern with *triclinium* (e) and wine-jars (f): (2) the garden (B) in a small-house plot behind a tavern (A, that of Euxinus). C marks the entrance to his house, with its own garden behind.

the rose-garden with the small vineyard and its terrace at the end, and everything from the area of the fish-tank and its culvert as far as the yard; and the yard with its buildings and the storehouse and the reservoirs on the terrace, and from the area of the terrace as far as the reedbed, including all the paths as they are marked out: one *iugerum* [about 0.25 ha] all told.[6]

(For a vivid illustration of the layout of estates like this, see fig. 44). These tomb-inscriptions are a very valuable source for the nature of the peripheries of Roman cities, and Rome itself in particular; with or without the funerary function, they were fragmented into tiny intensively farmed lots which also fulfilled the needs of *amoenitas*.

Such places, even when tinier still, could combine house and garden, tomb and country estate, all in one sentimental expression, as with the lot of the freedman doctor Hostius Pamphilus and his wife: 'This is our eternal home, this is our farm, these are our gardens, this is our monument'.[7] The plot was 13 × 24 feet.

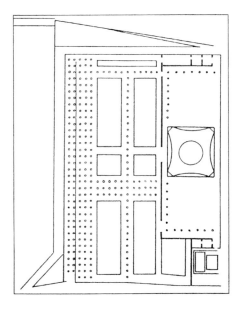

Fig. 44: Plan of a kepotaphion (garden-tomb) from the neighbourhood of Rome, now in Urbino. The tomb is the circular structure: also marked are (probably) beds, individual vines and a reedbed (*harundinetum*), as well as the public access.

III. Dwellers in paradise

The tomb-garden introduces us to a wider dimension of garden-making. So far, the productive element has been stressed, and that is right in a world where the means of survival were always precarious and the places where water was available in sufficient abundance to make a garden were not to be squandered. But there were cultural traditions alongside Romulus' vegetable patch which we need to take into account. The tomb-garden was usually known by the Greek term *kepotaphion*, and it was from the east that many of its associations derived; probably the most famous instance of the type is, after all, the place near Golgotha where 'there was a garden, and in the garden a new sepulchre, wherein was never man yet laid'.[8]

In the east, the principal garden type had been the enclosed watered orchard equipped for both pleasure and production: the *paradeisos*. This is quite different from the tradition that we have been examining so far. That tradition depended on subdivision, fragmentation, sharing within the community; the *paradeisos* was the demesne of a great man, his *temenos*, like the lots of the great rulers in the Homeric poems: those of Glaucus and Sarpedon on the banks of the Xanthus in Lycia or the orchards of Laertes above the town of Ithaca, a sign of his standing and personal private exclusive power and privilege.[9] The paradises of the Persian nobility and above all of the kings of the Fertile Crescent lands were domestic in the sense that they were abodes as well as hunting parks, scenes for the setting of entertainments, or places for the production of exotic foodstuffs. They could also be demonstrations of power and skill, where they were formed or maintained through sophisticated hydraulic engineering in places where lush fertility was uncharacteristic of the natural environment.

The citizen egalitarianism of the Greek and Roman city was always uneasily balanced against the tendency to acquire wealth and status and their visible signs on the part of the powerful few, and it is not surprising that the imitation of the paradise garden is found quite early in Greek history, or that it soon penetrated to the Roman elite as that acquired more experience in the symbolism of world rule with the conquests of the late third and second centuries B.C.

At this period we find the genesis of the Roman villa. In the Italian countryside the Roman elite and their imitators began to build substantial country houses as centres of estates where the productive landscape could be managed in an efficient, imaginative, flexible and varied way to provide the proprietor with a good return from the sale of produce. It was inevitable that such an estate would have a place for garden cultivation. The Elder Cato, whose advice on the establishment of villas of this sort was composed in the middle of the second century B.C., considered irrigated gardens second only to high-yield vineyards as a source of profit.[10]

From the start there was a tendency for the villa to be a comfortable dwelling too, and the adaptation of the amenities of the dwelling to the particular portfolio of productive advantages of each villa location became an amusing pastime for villa-owners, which reached great complexity and sophistication by the last years of the Republic. A coastal villa with wet vineyard behind the coastal dunes, like the tiny plot which produced the celebrated Caecuban wine, or fisheries which made use of the rocks and pools of a cliff coast, offered different opportunities for setting up a dining-room or a retiring place where the picturesque side of your productive activity could be savoured. Inland, a gazebo with a view over your ploughed fields or olive terraces could be worth contriving.

If you had green pastures in the valley bottom, those made a good adjunct to the design, and the water-supply that made possible certain crucial aspects of the life of leisure, such as bathing, could be used also to produce a planted garden-plot which made a paradisal setting for domestic life, with rivulets, fountains, and specimen trees. These recurred in other combinations—with fishponds or aviaries, sometimes with preserves of game animals—but the point was still the art of living graciously in your personal productive landscape.

The aviary usually provided *delectatio* at some remove from the dining-room, but it is revealing that some Romans felt impelled to try to fill the gap:

> Lucullus intended a third kind of aviary [besides the functional and the ornamental]: the combined type, which he tried out at his villa at Tusculum. In the same building as the bird-house, he had an enclosed *triclinium* where he could regularly take his elegant meals and see some birds on the serving-dish, cooked, and others fluttering round the windows, caught. No good. The birds flying inside the windows give less pleasure than the intrusive smell, filling the nostrils, gives annoyance.[11]

IV. The inhabited vegetable garden

The natural location for the villa was away from the city, sometimes even in a wild or inaccessible place like some of the sea coasts. However, by the first century B.C. a specialised form of the domestic garden that we have been describing appeared, which was just as adaptive to the circumstances of its location, but in a new type of setting—the fringes of the town (the suburban zone is graphically illustrated on the famous relief from Avezzano, fig. 45).[12]

Several factors were in play. It was convenient to have the amenities of a country house in the neighbourhood of the political and economic business of the city. More people could see your magnificence and it was more expensive to buy land, so you made more of a splash. You could do things on a suburban estate that there was no room for in a town house, some of which might be advantageous in troubled times.

We should not underestimate the simple fact that it was a potent sign of how little you cared for the traditional proprieties to extend the display of personal might and villa-owner's swagger into the fringes of the citizen world, buying up the lots of the suburbs in their dozens to construct a convenient paradise just for you. To drive the point home you called the new estate 'market gardens' (horti). As Pliny the Elder said:

> Now under the name vegetable gardens they own pleasure-grounds, farms and country-houses in the city itself. The first person ever to do this was that instructor in leisure activities Epicurus, at Athens: until his time there had not been any custom of living in the country in the town.[13]

It took the emperor Nero to go one further and encroach on the city itself with his own remarkable suburban villa, the Golden House (cf. p. 97 above). But the outraged reactions to that project confirm that the messages of ruthless power over the landscape intended by the owners of such estates were fully understood.[14]

Like the villa garden, the horti needed to adapt their decor to their location. Their dining-rooms and bowers should reveal the suburban location without suffering from inconveniences such as noise or dirt. Take the gardens of Iulius Martialis high on the Janiculum hill outside Rome: the pleasure of the view lay in the scene of the Tiber and its traffic, and the bustle on the Via Flaminia, but both were safely out of earshot.[15] Recent research has disclosed another fine example: the garden estate of Augustus' equestrian confidant Maecenas, a part of the ruins of which has been known since the nineteenth century.[16] An elegant hall, which was interpreted as an auditorium when the site was first explored, lies across the Republican city walls of Rome (see fig. 46): not out of simple perversity; approaching from within the city, the astonished guest found himself unexpectedly confronted with the view

Fig. 45: Drawing of a relief from near Avezzano, depicting a city and its neighbourhood: note the suburban villa (see n.12).

uninterrupted by the fortification, across a downward sweep of the suburban countryside opening out for miles across the Campagna to the distant ranges of the Apennines.

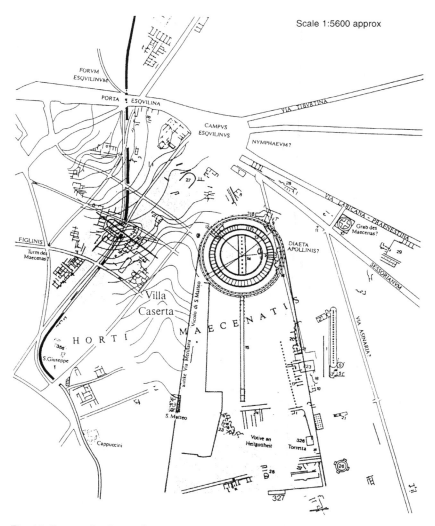

Fig. 46: Rome: Gardens of Maecenas. Plan of the neighbourhood of the Horti Maecenatiani, showing the location of the 'Auditorium' on the city wall and its orientation.

Fig. 47: Rome: Gardens of Maecenas. The 'Auditorium' as first discovered.

The complex enjoyed further wide views in the other direction—it is on the highest point of the site of Rome—over the city itself: the buildings included a tall tower, infamous because it was from here that Nero was believed to have watched the destruction of his capital during the great fire of A.D. 64. The location between the city and the countryside was central to the themes of the design. When Maecenas laid out the *horti*, he converted a stretch of the old city wall into a terrace amid orchards.[17]

In country villas, the massing of the buildings made them look like little cities, and the decor of their gardens sometimes alluded to this whimsically by making the boundary wall a miniature city fortification complete with turrets (fig. 48). The idea that the house, for good or—mostly—ill, was comparable in size with a whole town, was a widespread one, and celebrated in the language of paradox: 'people like you have the territories of whole cities as your country estates and fill up cities with your houses, while within your buildings you enclose the waves and the forests'.[18]

On the other side of the city from Maecenas' property, other estates of this kind played with their location in different ways. The most famous is the complex of the Horti Caesaris, in the district that is now called Monteverde, where Julius Caesar entertained Cleopatra on her visit to Rome in 44 B.C. Another episode tells us a good deal about the sort of hospitality that was afforded by these rather specialised domestic settings. When Caesar returned to Rome after Munda in late 45 B.C. he held a grand *salutatio* for the *plebs* here: they were gathered in what must have been a great peristyle, and came forward to greet the dictator, who was standing in the space between two columns of a great portico. What they could see and he could not was that in the adjacent intercolumniation a notorious rabble-rouser, who claimed to be the long-lost son of Marius, was making his own communications to Caesar's audience, and stealing the limelight, being greeted with almost the same enthusiasm.[19] The advantages of possessing an estate large enough and close enough to Rome to provide mass hospitality and deliver political messages were clear: when Caesar left the property to be public land in his will, he was capitalising on memories of the extent to which as a popular leader he had literally made the people feel at home in his lavish suburban residence, a gesture which was sometimes repeated by his successors in their *horti* and villas.

The location of Caesar's Horti was such that they commanded the Tiber bank from terraces on the slope of the Janiculum, from which Rome appeared upstream. Nearer the city, villas on the bank of the river

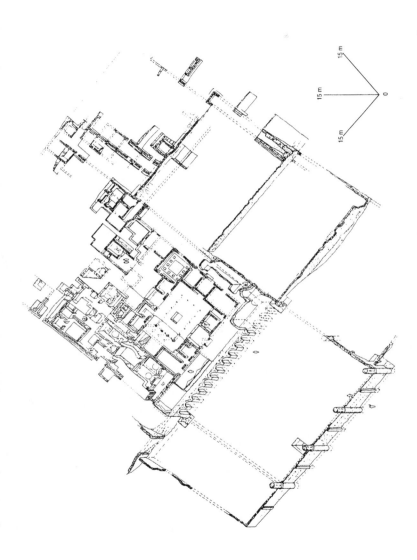

15 m

15 m

15 m

0

Fig. 48: The boundary wall of the garden of the villa at Settefinestre in Etruria, in the form of a miniature city wall.

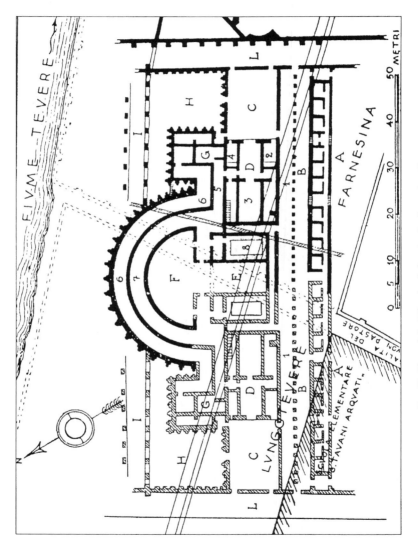

Fig. 49: Plan of the Tiber-bank *horti* at La Farnesina, Rome.

looked across to the suburban monuments of the Campus Martius and to the skyline of the city itself. We know the names of several proprietors of *horti* in this location: Catullus' mistress Clodia, Augustus' ally Agrippa; but only one has been explored, that under the Renaissance pleasance of La Farnesina (fig. 49). Once again, as a visitor progressed through the spaces of the building, there was a constant sense of surprise as *cryptoporticus* gave way to *viridiarium* and beyond that, suddenly, the view across the Tiber to the Campus Martius was opened up.

The world of production which was deployed as a decorative element here was of course the small-scale production of the lots of the city periphery, but reinterpreted: luxury crops, seasonal oddities, the full range of the enterprises that the Romans called, with the same wit that we see in the name *horti*, 'villa pasturing' (*pastio villatica*). Best of all, though, was the demonstration that the owner of such a place could afford, unlike the toiling owners of the *kepotaphia* or even the proprietors of country villas, to plant trees and shrubs which were of no economic use whatsoever. The truly ornamental garden was born from the excitement of being able to show off water, rich soil, a location near the market, an abundant labour force—and deliberately chosen and soignée sterility.

V. Nature as domestic artifice

The Roman garden aimed at responding to the landscape around. That was the creation of Nature, and the garden was, even more than the architecture of the house itself, the place where the intentions and abilities of the owner came into contact with the dispositions of Nature, and found itself modifying and improving them. That was, after all, how cultivation itself was seen to work, and it was only a small step from the creative adaptation of natural order that is involved in production to other demonstrations of the potency of human *ingenium* and *ars*. In the Persian tradition, that often took the form of landscape architecture on a grand scale, which goes beyond our subject-matter here: the terraces, tunnels, artificial watercourses, lakes, bridges and dams of the more ambitious Roman villas, turning land into sea and vice versa; the type of domestic—if that is the right adjective—architecture that earned Lucullus the sobriquet 'Xerxes in a toga'.[20] Such grand projects had their pale reflection in the waterworks or landscaping of much smaller gardens, in which another relatively accessible practice was the cultivation of plants for their own sake, even when they yielded no saleable or useful product. For the grander gardener, this was part of a repertoire of forms of ostentatious display of horticultural sophistication, with exotic species, cold frames, water-lifting devices and so on.

The plane tree was a characteristic example of an introduction which served only for ornament and shade: 'who can fail to be astonished, perfectly reasonably, at the fact that a tree has been introduced from an alien world just for its shadow?'.[21] But there was a much wider range of evergreen plants grown as shrubs or for ground cover, the object of which was to fashion cool and refreshing spaces where there had been none before. These played a conspicuous part in the mainstream tradition of Roman gardening which was to achieve through artifice 'the semblance of what Nature had denied', as Tacitus memorably puts it in the case of the *ne plus ultra* of the style, Nero's Golden House.[22] The plane, after all, was an exotic; its very presence in a Roman garden suggested the power that had enabled trees from the homeland of the paradise garden to be introduced to Italy. Some of these plants were difficult to cultivate, and the provision of what they needed offered opportunities for the display of virtuoso technique, like running a successful fish-pond or dormouse-breedery; one enthusiast is supposed to have watered a favourite plane tree, unnecessarily but revealingly, with wine as a sign of his diligent care. But it was in their unproductiveness that they really excelled; only a person of tremendous taste, vast wealth, and highly cultured insouciance would devote the most fertile productive locations to the purely aesthetic and pleasurable.

Roman landscape architecture, then, centred on a taste for evoking place, either by creating an atmosphere of elsewhere or by reinforcing and responding to what was around. It was, indeed, called 'place-art' (*ars topiaria*), the phrase from which we derive the term of more limited reference that describes the trimmed hedges which were one small part of the repertoire of the Roman *topiarius*.[23] This artificiality and its expense were frequently condemned by Roman moral writers, and much of our information derives from their disapproving, and usually very rhetorical, descriptions of the excesses of the technique. But it was partly because it was so controversial that the practice was so lively and vigorous an art form, and it is important for us to attempt to understand why it mattered so much.

VI. Interiors and exteriors

In terms of 'place-art', then, the relationship of the Roman formal garden to the house takes on a new significance. It will serve to make statements about the setting of the property, and the extent to which the

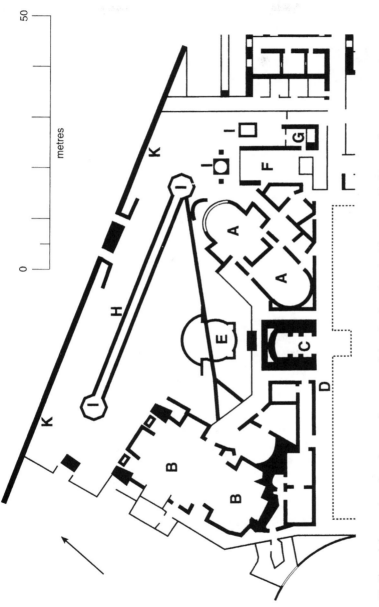

Fig. 50: Plan of the remains of gardens on the terrace of the 'Greek and Latin Libraries' at Hadrian's Villa. A. tower 1 ('Latin Library'); B. tower 2 ('Greek Library'); C. Republican *nymphaeum*; D. peristyle; E. *triconchos* room; F. oecus; G. latrine; H. Euripus channel; I. fountains; K. terrace wall.

designer of the domestic architecture wants to assert or subvert that location. We have now seen the three principal strands of raw material in the design process: the back-door kitchen plot, the edge of the built-up town, and the management of Nature. These could all be manipulated in the interests of *ars topiaria*.

The villa that was situated out in the deep countryside would typically stress its location through the laying out of views which looked away from the property towards the local settlement or town, to emphasise the distance and the separation. In the Campagna, the distant view of Rome was a particularly important focal point for external terraces and garden spaces of this sort. At Hadrian's Villa at Tivoli (cf. p. 107 above), the terrace-garden in front of the pavilion *triclinia* which used to be called the 'Greek and Latin Libraries' (fig. 50) is laid out in what looks a highly irregular way, with waterworks and paths at strange angles, until the location looking across the intervening miles to the distant city is appreciated.[24] Then the way in which varied framing and focusing of this vista from the different dining facilities of this part of the complex is achieved becomes clearer. From another part of the villa another, more formal terrace is clearly oriented to frame the view of Tivoli itself, picturesquely perched on the Apennine scarp (pl. 22).

We have seen how the *horti* of the suburban zone combine this sense of open space and extrovert architecture with some of the closer-knit design and interior management of the town-house lot. Vitruvius coined the term *villa pseudo-urbana* for the design in which, in a halfway stage between the villa and the town house, the normal order of *atrium* and peristyle was reversed and visitors arrived first in the latter, perhaps the situation described in the anecdote of Caesar's *horti* quoted above.[25]

Even in the lot in the town itself where there was room left over from the house, the garden ground could be beautified by enclosing it in a regular portico on one or more sides—the peristyle that has long been seen as a standard feature of the Pompeian-type house. The way in which such places have been planted by the archaeological management of Pompeii is however quite misleading; recent work has conclusively shown that, instead of low plantings, these spaces, which were after all primarily designed for summer shade, were often sheltered by two or three enormous plane-trees which extended the canopy of the roof of the peristyle.[26]

At Hadrian's Villa at Tivoli, detailed examination of the complex traditionally known as the 'Garden Stadium' has revealed a really elaborate example of how this tradition, as it is simply seen at Pompeii,

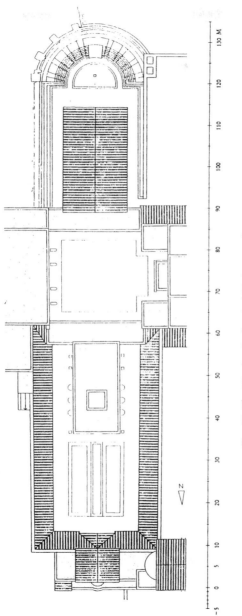

Fig. 51: The 'Garden Stadium' of Hadrian's Villa at Tivoli.

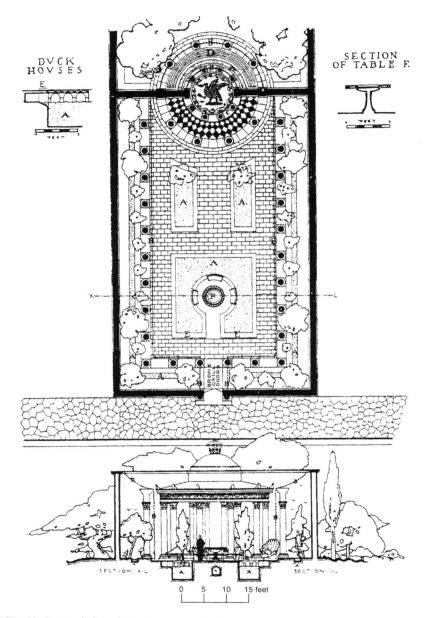

Fig. 52: Restored plan of Varro's aviary at Casinum.

could be developed.[27] The structure is an elongated court, with columned porches opening into it from three directions. But as an exterior space it is compromised in two important ways. It is surrounded by walls, overlooked and dominated by the masses of palatial building alongside (and is indeed intended to be viewed from above as well as being experienced from within); and it is nearly filled by pavilions, between which the planted spaces—one sequence of hexagonal basins for specimen shrubs and two raised flower-beds—are reduced to the role of alternations in the multiple sequence of different kinds of oblique light and shade that a person strolling along or across the courtyard would experience (fig. 51). One end is curved, with stepped tiers for the support of more portable *viridia*; the effect is also to introduce allusions to other superficially similar structures like theatres or the curved end of a circus. Another structure of this sort is found in the 'Auditorium' of the Horti Maecenatiani.[28]

The hexagonal tubs introduce us to an important Roman concept in this field. They are for *viridia* ('green things'), the Roman name for specimen plants, and their location is therefore a *viridiarium*, a place for *viridia*.[29]

As with a conservatory or orangery in a country house of the eighteenth century, the *viridiarium* was a place in which the best of horticulture could be juxtaposed with the amenities of indoors. It was a place in which the activities of the domestic space, particularly the ceremonious Roman meal, could comfortably take place; though, as we have seen, the practice of dining in gardens, even in the very small ones associated with tombs or the rather rustic ones in taverns in the periphery of cities like Pompeii, was widely diffused, and the elaborate garden *triclinium* was part of the same repertoire as the *viridiarium*, which had the advantage of being pleasant in cooler weather. In the *viridiarium* the function of particularly exquisite plants as ornaments made a different use of the ambiguity between growing and made decoration, and the play between enclosed domestic room and outdoor air worked in a different way from how it did in the peristyle or garden along the side of the house. Varro's aviary, once again, provides an instance of the ambiguous effect (fig. 52). Although most *viridia* were purely ornamental, a setting like this could be used for the celebration of the production of some particularly exotic rarity, such as citron. Recent work at the villa of Herod the Great near Jericho has revealed a carefully planted peristyle-*viridiarium* which may be one of the balsam groves mentioned in the literary sources (fig. 53).[30]

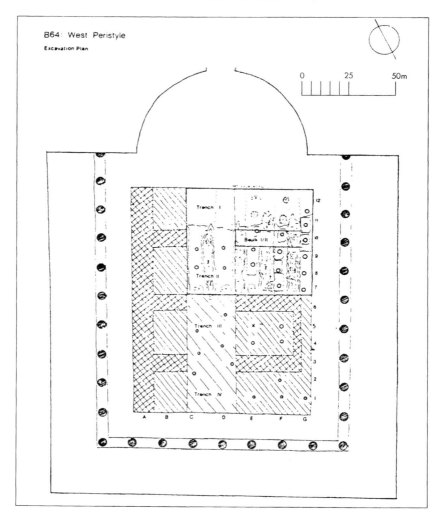

Fig. 53: The planted peristyle of the villa of Herod the Great at Jericho.

This, finally, was another form of high taste which was thought to have got out of hand in the evil days of the emperor Nero; at least in their very nature such places had usually been small. Pliny contrasts the good old days when two *iugera* each was enough for the Roman People, and it gave no measure to anyone larger than this—with which no member of Nero's household would have been satisfied, a year or two ago, as a site for a *viridiarium*. They actually had a penchant for ponds of this size, and it is only a matter of chance that no-one built kitchens to match.[31]

The passage confirms how specialised and concentrated the luxury of the *viridiarium* was.

VI. Games with materials

The king made a feast unto all the people that were present in Shusan the palace, both unto great and small, seven days, in the court of the garden of the king's palace; where were white, green, and blue hangings, fastened with cords of fine linen and purple to silver rings and pillars of marble: the beds were of gold and silver, upon a pavement of red, and blue, and white, and black marble. And they gave them drink in vessels of gold . . . and royal wine in abundance.[32]

Paradise was not the only legacy of the Fertile Crescent to the high culture of Greece and Rome. The Persian kings, as we see from this biblical anecdote of Xerxes, were tent-dwellers, and that was reflected in the architecture of their permanent palaces. The tent is more a way of operating than a fixed structural form, as we see clearly here; in the life of luxury, it takes the form of the deployment in existing spaces of draperies, awnings and hangings of the precious textiles whose near total loss has done so much to impoverish our visual understanding of the ancient world. The literary and visual evidence gives us only a hint of the importance of the shows of cloth, on temple porticoes, or in fixed buildings, or in places of public spectacle where the management of the huge weights of fabric was itself part of the wonder and spectacle.

The importance of textiles, as of other portable furnishings in inlaid wood or decorative metal, lay in their temporary, adaptable nature. We are inclined to think of architecture as an art of permanence and solidity, and that is encouraged by the masses of masonry and brick which have survived as the most impressive examples of Roman building. But Roman domestic design, in garden spaces as in houses of all kinds, was an architecture of the mutable, and this was actually conceived of as deliberately contrasting with the permanence of works of grand public importance. When a prominent senator rebuilt his house at Rome with excessive elaboration and care, Augustus mocked him by saying 'Building like this you cheer me up, because you suggest that Rome really will be eternal'.[33]

The architectural enthusiast, the *aedificator*, was used to being more thoroughly involved in the specifications of his new domestic architecture than is easily imaginable to us. The materials with which the rooms were made and finished were chosen with much more care than the relatively simple repertoire used in most interiors today, and those who experienced the effect were used to recognising what marbles or colours or precious woods had been used, and what their associations were. 'He pulls it down, puts it up again, changes right angles for curves', says Horace of an *aedificator*; constant fiddling with the visual effects was normal.[34] The negative side of this stagy decoration was the alleged risk of collapse, the peril of being crushed in the ruins of your finery by which the moral pundits of first century A.D. Rome found a punishment which fitted the crime of too self-indulgent a passion for the architecture of the mutable.[35]

The more realistic consequence was that Roman interiors became flexible backdrops for constructive reinterpretation and adaptation for the purposes and tastes of different social gatherings at different times of day or year, and especially for entertainment at meals, and it was to this process that the garden had an important contribution to make. The garden offered a new dimension of flexibility: soft and changing natural elements or open spaces and vistas could be substituted for any of the fixed, artificial, hard constituents of the ordinary interior.

Trees, shrubs, green-floored groves were extensions of an architecture which was wholly artificial, and could be shaped accordingly. The process was assisted by the widespread theory that the trabeated architecture of the orders itself derived from primitive adaptations of living or recently culled natural material.[36] Trees became columns; real columns and architectural members were swathed in ivies; shrubs were trimmed and clipped to make them resemble statues; low-growing plants could form inscribed names like the messages included in tessellated pavements. In the magnificent garden complex of the villa at Oplontis, statues, pillars in the portico and large plane trees march along the great *piscina* in the same rhythm, the furnishings assisting the ambiguity as to whether the boles of the trees or the columns are the primary architectural members (fig. 54).[37] In the porticoes of Varro's aviary the central row of columns was replaced by a row of low-growing dwarf shrubs.[38]

Xerxes' feast was in a garden, and there was a long tradition of the use of natural and man-made drapery to festoon the rich at their dining, embowering human activity. Pliny the Elder attacks those who hang red awnings up to screen excessive light from their moss-gardens.[39] In a garden room all the walls might be replaced by the dense foliage of a *nemus* or grove, the tree-trunks acting as columns; in the spaces temporary screens of textiles or woodwork or hanging foliage screened the occupant. The ceiling was formed of arbour-trellis, or the boughs of trees, or of awnings, or a mixture. The place might be an aviary with live birds in the trees. The floor—or even parts of the walls—might not even be solid, but water, rippling and reflecting dappled and changing light on the surfaces.[40] But all or some of these elements might turn out to be

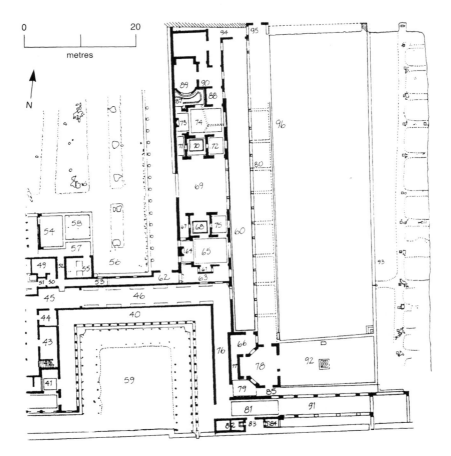

Fig. 54: Oplontis: Villa of the Poppaei. The south wing of the villa, to show plantings, furnishings, and architecture.

illusion, and actually fixed and artificial: the textiles or the grove itself might be a fresco, like the Prima Porta example (below, p. 149); the temporary partitions, or the birds, or some of the more picturesque serving staff—dwarfs, small children, slaves dressed as wild fishermen— might actually be rendered in immovable marble. Another list of the equipment of a *kepotaphion*, dated A.D. 6, makes the point well:

> a *triclinium* with a trellis and a pavement, a stone table with a base, a marble table, the aqueduct water tank with its pipes and three bronze taps, the fountainhead in the shape of a bronze lily, three seats, three benches, two square tables, a maple-wood table, travertine steps to the ossuary, the vines, the *viridia*.[41]

The wall-less house was an idea accessible to the Romans them- selves: Dio describes the baldachin over the bier in the funeral procession of the emperor Pertinax as being 'a columniated unwalled dwelling'.[42] The pavilions of a complex like the Garden Stadium of Hadrian's Villa were also intended to be transparent, roofed and columniated in solid masonry, but surrounded by the changing and semi-permanent speci- mens of a *viridiarium*. There were other halfway houses: you might make use of screens of columns which acted as divisions but which did not support a roof on either side, or solid walls whose layout was that of an apsidal room which was not roofed, like the 'Auditorium' in the Horti Maecenatiani.

In the mutable domestic architecture of ancient Rome, the tempo- rariness of beauty was itself a pleasure. In a Mediterranean climate, flowers were inevitably a highly transient part of garden art, restricted to a very brief springtime season despite efforts to prolong it or to induce second flowering. That did not prevent *violaria* and *rosaria* from being much admired. Nature had ordained certain patterns for plant life, and any modification that could be managed was a testimony to ingenuity and ultimately to power; so gardens were made on ships, or on the roofs of houses and the tops of towers, through irrigation in dry wildernesses, and shelter in exposed ones; the precarious survival of the enterprise made it the more estimable.

We are now in a position to consider a further curious development of Roman taste in the area where garden and domestic design meet: the cave.[43] The cave was a house of natural and morally respectable sim- plicity, a *domus secundum naturam*, and was believed like the groves and the huts that were evoked with arbours and bowers to have been an ancient type of dwelling.[44] It therefore had associations with rustic

Fig. 55: The 'Serapeum' *triclinium* of Hadrian's Villa, by Piranesi.

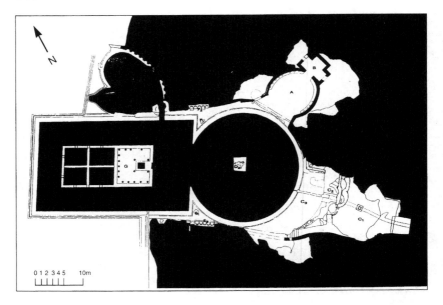

Fig. 56: The cave-*triclinium* of Tiberius' villa at Sperlonga.

simplicity, but also with religious awe, since gods and nymphs also dwelt in abodes of this kind. This gave it an appeal to the sense of a deep past tradition which we have already met when we introduced this discussion with what the Romans thought about the role of horticulture in their heroically simple origins. And the uncouth roughness of the cave offered splendid opportunities for domestication which overcame the squalor without concealing it: improving on the rock with stylised artificial rock, mounting decorative statues in the niches of the walls, transforming the darkness with light effects or water, or even constructing a cave with a stream running out of it under and around the dinner-tables, all completely artificial, as at the 'Serapeum' of Hadrian's Villa (fig. 55).

Some of the examples will be familiar. The *viridiarium* of the Horti Maecenatiani, approached down a ramp, turned out to be no tunnel or grotto but a sunken court, with the tremendous city-denying view that we have already discussed. The coastal palace of Tiberius at Sperlonga built a combination of landscaped dining-room, fish pond fed by the sea, and mythological tableau of scenes from the *Odyssey*, in an artfully improved natural sea-cave, with spectacular views out along the coast (fig. 56).[45] At the villa *Ad Gallinas Albas* at Prima Porta north of Rome the famous fresco of the bird-filled grove now in the Terme Museum in Rome (pl. 23) was the unexpected culmination of a descent which must have seemed bound to lead inevitably to an enclosed underground cavernous place rather than an illusion of forest.

VII. The problem of Roman gardening

What have we discovered as we have made the transition from the intensive horticulture of the Mediterranean landscape, through Roman ideas about their own past, to the incorporation in domestic architecture—in town, suburb and country—of the most highly sophisticated outgrowths of both productive horticulture and the wild, unproductive wilderness that denied it?

First, that the 'garden as domestic building' turns out not to be some minor aspect of the subject, but central: what we have explored has been intimately connected with domestic architecture at every point.

Second, and more unexpectedly, we have seen that Roman uses of the raw materials of what we would call 'gardening' or 'garden art' are much stranger than we might imagine, partly because they are so tightly bound up with the question of the nature of the house. The starting-points may be familiar—market gardening, or evocations of nature as a contrast to civilisation—but what the Romans did with them can perhaps hardly be called 'gardening' in the modern sense.

Third, we have perhaps begun to understand a little—through examples mainly from the heartland of Roman culture, and from the developments of the very highest elite—of the formation of a cultural tradition robust enough to be transmitted to the corners of the Empire, so that similar principles can be used to understand the gardens which archaeology reveals at Conimbriga (Coimbra) in Portugal or at Fishbourne in Britain. It is also a tradition which went on evolving in the Byzantine and Islamic traditions of landscape and domestic architecture, to cross-fertilise again in the late Middle Ages with what the west had remembered of Roman tradition itself.

Finally, we have seen that the literary tradition which, describing and reflecting on Roman practice, has preserved many Roman ideas for us to understand, is actually an integral part of the cultural phenomenon of domestic architecture itself; there can be no separating out of the study of Roman domestic architecture into aesthetic as opposed to practical, or philosophical as opposed to social and economic; the fascination of this subject is that the astonishing complexities and sophistication of

Roman high culture will only be unravelled by taking all of its dimensions into account together.

NOTES

1. Catullus 62.39–40.

2. Pliny, *Natural History* 19.49–56 is a key passage for this.

3. Pliny, *Natural History* 19.59.

4. W. Jashemski, *The Gardens of Pompeii* (New Rochelle, NY 1979), ch. 8.

5. On tomb-gardens, N. Purcell, 'Tomb and suburb', in H. von Hesberg and P. Zanker (eds), *Römische Gräberstraßen* (Munich 1987), 25–41.

6. *CIL* XI 3895.

7. *CIL* VI 9583.

8. John 19.41.

9. Homer, *Iliad* 12.310–14; *Odyssey* 24, esp. 336–44.

10. *De agricultura* 1.7.

11. Varro, *De re rustica* 3.4.3. For Varro's own better arrangements, ibid. 3.5.8–17.

12. For the relief, *Antike Denkmäler* III 3 (1914–15), p. 32 and plate 31; or A. Geffroy, 'L'archéologie du lac Fucin', *Revue Archéologique*. 1878 II, 1–11. The best treatment of the *horti* is still P. Grimal, *Les jardins de Rome*, 2nd edition (Paris 1969).

13. Pliny, *Natural History* 19.50–51.

14. For *rus in urbe*, N. Purcell, 'Town in country and country in town', in E. MacDougall (ed.), *The Ancient Roman Villa-Garden* (Washington D.C. 1988), 185–203.

15. Martial 4.64.

16. C. Häuber, 'Zur Topographie der Horti Maecenatis und der Horti Lamiani auf dem Esquilin in Rom', *Kölner Jahrbuch* 23 (1990), 11–107.

17. Horace, *Satires* 1.8.14. Nero and the fire, Suetonius, *Nero* 38.2.

18. Seneca, *Controversiae* 5.5.1.

19. Valerius Maximus 9.15.1.

20. Velleius Paterculus 2.33.4; Plutarch, *Lucullus* 39.3.

21. Pliny, *Natural History* 12.6.

22. *Annals* 15.42.

23. Grimal, *Les jardins de Rome*, 88–95.

24. F. Rakob, 'Ambivalente Apsiden—zur Zeichensprache der römischen Architektur', *Römische Mitteilungen* 94 (1987), 1–28.

25. Vitruvius, *De architectura* 6.5.3. A well-known example is the Villa of the Mysteries outside the walls of Pompeii.

26. Jashemski, *Gardens of Pompeii*, ch. 2.

27. A. Hoffmann, *Das Gartenstadion in der Villa Hadriana* (Mainz 1980).

28. That a parallel with a theatre is intended is demonstrated by Varro's use of the term *theatridion* for this sort of configuration in his aviary, *De re rustica* 3.5.13.

29. The spelling *viridarium* is misleading, as is the frequency with which the word is used by those drawing plans of Roman houses: the ordinary word for a garden plot is simply *hortus*: *viridiaria* are special, the term technical.

30. K.L. Gleason, personal communication. For the palace and balsam-groves, Josephus *Bellum Judaicum* 4, 362, 468; Strabo 16, 241, and E. Netzer, 'The Hasmonean and Herodian winter palaces at Jericho', *Israel Exploration Journal* 25 (1975), 89–100.

31. Pliny, *Natural History* 18.7.

32. *Esther* 1.5–7.

33. Plutarch *Moralia* 208 (*Regum et Imperatorum Apophthegmata, Caesar Augustus* 15), on the house of 'Piso'.

34. Horace, *Epistles* 1.1.100.

35. See especially Seneca, *Epistulae morales* 90, 41–4.

36. See, famously, Vitruvius *De architectura* 2.1.2, with J. Rykwert, *On Adam's House in Paradise* (New York 1972).

37. For Oplontis, W. Jashemski, 'Recently excavated gardens and cultivated land of the villas at Boscoreale and Oplontis', in MacDougall (ed.), *The Ancient Roman Villa-Garden* 31–75.

38. Varro, *De re rustica* 3.5.11.

39. Pliny, *Natural History* 19.24.

40. Statius, *Silvae* 1.3.17–19 on water reflecting trees in Manilius Vopiscus' villa at Tivoli: 'the deceiving reflection makes reply to the branches above' (*fallax responsat imago frondibus*).

41. *Année epigraphique* 1986.25.

42. Dio 75.4.2, *oikema atoichon peristylon*.

43. H. Lavagne, *Operosa antra: recherches sur la grotte à Rome de Sylla à Hadrien* (Rome 1988) will be the standard work for some time.

44. Pliny *Natural History* 7.194.

45. A.F. Stewart, 'To entertain an emperor: Sperlonga, Laokoon and Tiberius at the dinner-table', *Journal of Roman Studies* 67 (1977), 76–90.

6

Military Housing

DAVID P. DAVISON

It may be thought surprising to extend consideration of Roman domestic buildings to the military context; such a decision can, however, be justified by the primary importance of the military in the Roman world, by the great numbers of men accommodated in permanent or semi-permanent military installations throughout the Empire, and by the degree to which military buildings incorporated features of the classical Mediterranean monumental and domestic building traditions. Indeed, to exclude the military would be to overlook the prime mover in the shaping of monumental and civic building, at least in the formative years of the frontier provinces of the Empire.

Under Augustus, the Roman army achieved substantially the form and organisation which it was to retain until the reforms of Diocletian at the close of the third century; also under Augustus the process of inexorable expansion of the Roman Empire came to a halt and the army became increasingly attached to a series of permanent or semi-permanent bases which delineated the extent of the Roman world. In contrast with the marching camps and short-stay installations of the Republic (and of the various military campaigns of the succeeding centuries), the early Principate saw the establishment of three principal kinds of military emplacement which remained characteristic of the Empire until the reforms at the end of the third century: the legionary fortress, the auxiliary fort and the fortlet. The fortress, some 20 to 25 ha in area, housed a legion of some five thousand infantrymen, Roman citizens all (fig. 57); the auxiliary fort, varying in size broadly between 1 and 4 ha, housed a unit (or units) of the auxiliary forces, be they cavalry, infantry or mixed infantry and cavalry, and accommodated between five hundred and one thousand men (and often their horses) (fig. 58); the fortlet was much smaller and often held fewer than one hundred auxiliaries in an installation of, typically, 0.10 ha (figs 59, 60). The auxiliaries, in general, received Roman citizenship only on honourable discharge after twenty-five years service. Truth does admit some complication of this schema in that fortresses also often housed a number of auxiliary troops and forts sometimes included legionaries in their complement, while garrisons often did not comprise whole units; but the general structure is clear.

The garrisons of these installations comprised the whole gamut of Roman army personnel, from the senatorial legionary commander in north Africa to the auxiliary infantryman undertaking his guard duty in a milecastle on Hadrian's Wall in northern Britain (cf. pl. 29). It is a measure of the system which governed the Roman army that the buildings in which these two operated and lived, although immensely different in degree, were linked by patterns of organisation, layout and construction, patterns which would have been readily apparent to both of them. As is not unusual in armies, so with the Roman army, the higher the soldier in the command structure, the more likely he was to occupy a building with which he would have been familiar in civilian life. Only at the lowest level of organisation did functional needs determine building form; nevertheless, even here, the Roman soldier's accommodation had elements of structure and furnishing fully redolent of the Classical and Mediterranean domestic tradition, no matter how inappropriate some of this may have been to the further-flung reaches of the Empire.

At the head of the legion was the *legatus legionis*, the legionary legate. The legate was usually a senator who had been praetor (at least from the Flavian period) and typically was in his early thirties. The legate held command of the legion for about three years; and successful tenure would lead to the prefecture of a Treasury at Rome or to the governorship of a small province. During his tour of duty the legate was accommodated in a veritable palace, the *praetorium*. The *praetorium* was situated adjacent to the *principia*, the headquarters and chief administrative building at the centre of the fortress. The *praetorium* was in fact a whole complex of buildings; it comprised substantial private apartments as well as accommodation for a large staff and facilities for official entertainment on a considerable scale. The legate was inevitably from a wealthy family and the size of his establishment enabled him to transport his whole family and household, with tableware and furnishings, and to continue to live in a style not far removed from his customary one.

INCHTUTHIL : GENERAL PLAN OF THE LEGIONARY FORTRESS

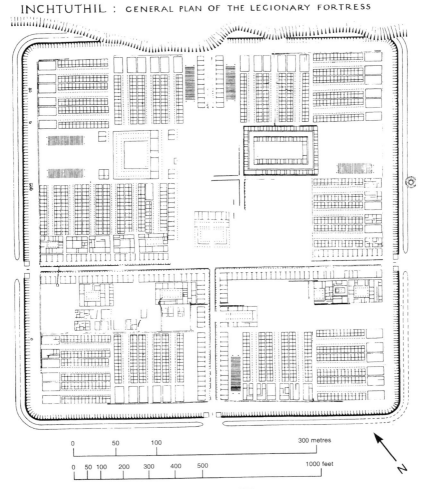

Fig. 57: Inchtuthil: legionary fortress, A.D. 83–86/87.

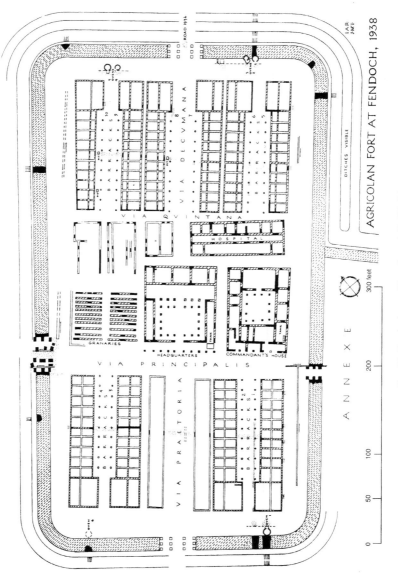

Fig. 58: Fendoch: auxiliary fort, A.D. 82–86.

AGRICOLAN FORT AT FENDOCH, 1938

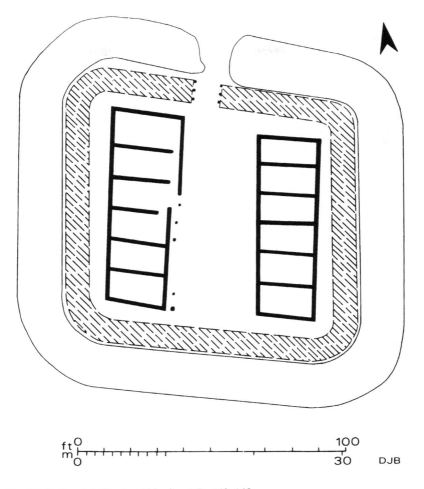

Fig. 59: Barburgh Mill: plan of fortlet, A.D. 142–148.

The best-known and most spectacular example of the legionary *praetorium* is at Vetera (fig. 61). Vetera was a double legionary fortress and thus contained two legates' palaces for the respective commanders. The larger of the two *praetoria* (76 × 94 m) was planned round a central open court with a wide opening from the street on one side and a large *triclinium* (dining-room) on the other. On the other sides were suites of rooms presumably for receiving guests. At the rear was a colonnaded

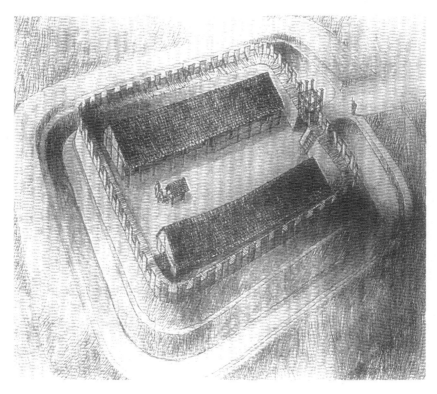

Fig. 60: Barburgh Mill: reconstruction of fortlet, A.D. 142–148.

garden with rounded ends, 82 × 18 m. The concept of the palace was of a number of open courts surrounded by ranges of rooms. The chief feature of interest in such buildings (and this is true of all legionary fortresses, even if less spectacularly so than Vetera) is the use, in the military context, of this Classical Mediterranean style of house with all the characteristic features such as hypocausts, mosaics and wall-painting.

Immediately junior to the legionary legate were the six military tribunes. One post was reserved for a senator designate and the remaining five for men of equestrian status. The tribunes were all provided with separate houses some 45 m square, which again commonly took the form of ranges of rooms grouped round a central courtyard and which were situated in the central forward part of the fortress. Where the plans of a number of tribunes' houses from the same fortress are known, they show slight variation in size and differences in the detailed organisation of their rooms. This may reflect the variety of social status and function of the tribunes (fig. 62).

It was equestrians who had the command of the auxiliary units. From the reign of Nero, or at least from the Flavian period, it was usual

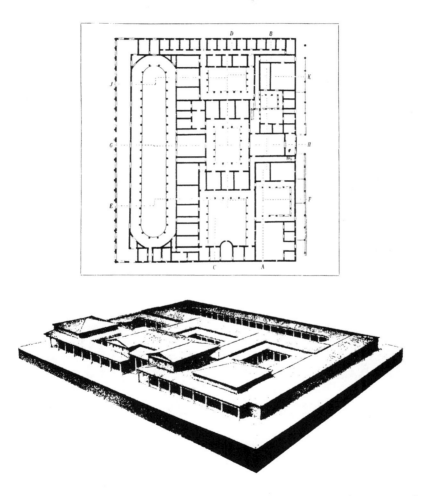

Fig. 61: Vetera I *praetorium*. Period 3, A.D. 46–69. Plan (scale 1:2160) and reconstructed model.

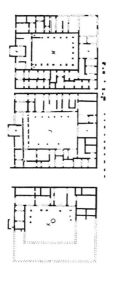

a

0   20
|—————|
   metres

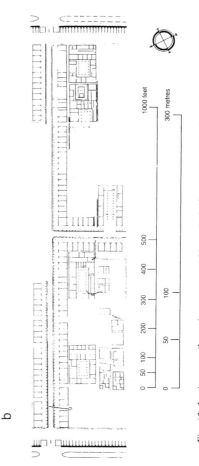

b

1000 feet

300 metres

0   50 100   200   300   400   500
0   50   100

Fig. 62: Legionary tribunes' quarters: (a) Vetera I. Scale 1:1730; (b) Inchtuthil. Scale 1:4000.

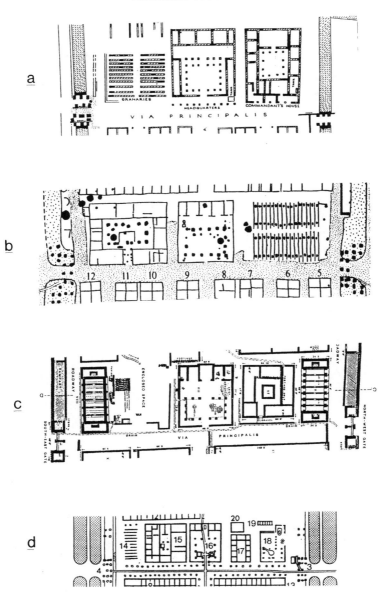

Fig. 63: Praetoria in auxiliary forts: (a) Fendoch; (b) Elginhaugh; (c) Gelligaer II; (d) Hofheim.

to serve first as *praefectus cohortis* (i.e. in charge of a unit of auxiliary infantry), second as *tribunus militum legionis*, and third as *praefectus equitum* (i.e. in charge of a unit of auxiliary cavalry). It is notable that the *praetoria* of the auxiliary forts, if rather smaller, correspond in many ways to the tribunes' houses in the fortresses (fig. 63). The *praetorium* comprised four ranges of rooms grouped around a central courtyard and the overall size was typically 20 × 20 m; its usual position was in the central range of fort buildings next to the fort *principia*. Although it is impossible to define the purpose of many of the rooms, it is probable that the large room usually found directly opposite the main entrance and across the open courtyard was the *triclinium*. Occasionally kitchens, latrines and bathing facilities have been identified, while remains of hypocausts, painted plaster and window glass give glimpses of the standard of life enjoyed.

The *praetorium* of the auxiliary fort was sufficient for the needs of the commanding officer's household which presumably, as finds at Vindolanda have shown,[1] included his immediate family and their domestic servants. Members of his personal staff may also have had offices and even living quarters in the premises. Guest rooms were also probably provided for visiting officials. The plans of the *praetoria* closely resembled civilian houses of comparable size, and parallels can be found in the courtyard plans of many provincial town houses. The courtyard ground-plan was developed in the warmer Mediterranean climate to provide welcome shade, yet it still proved valuable in the British and German fortresses and forts to give seclusion and privacy. The *praetorium* was essentially a private dwelling and tended to be less stereotyped in its internal arrangements than other fortress and fort buildings.

The rest of those who required accommodation (apart from servants, whose presence and housing is surrounded by much uncertainty) were the legionary centurions and legionaries in the fortresses and the auxiliary centurions and decurions (hereafter collectively referred to as officers) accompanied by their auxiliary infantry *centuriae* and cavalry *turmae* respectively in the forts and fortlets. All these men were housed in barracks which took up much of the remaining available space in their respective installations. The ten cohorts of the legion were divided into six centuries of eighty men. The six centuries of the cohort were accommodated (usually) in three facing pairs of barracks and the cohort groups of barracks were generally disposed round the perimeter of the fortress (see fig. 57). The much smaller numbers in the auxiliary forts were also housed in facing pairs of barracks, the pairs evenly distributed in the fort interior (see fig. 58). The troops in the fortlets were housed in small single or paired buildings which occasionally took the form of a single centurial barrack divided into two facing halves (fig. 64).

In contrast to the courtyard houses with their civilian antecedents described above, the barracks developed empirically. They can be seen to have derived from the layout of the tents of the century in the marching camp. In the first extant chapter of his *De Munitionibus Castrorum*, pseudo-Hyginus, writing either at the end of the first century or towards the end of the second, describes the manner in which eight tents of the ten eight-man tent groups or *contubernia* (two were on guard duty) of the century were set out in a line with, at one end, the centurion's larger tent. In front of the tents was a space for placing the soldiers' weapons and then in front of that again was a space for baggage and animals.[2]

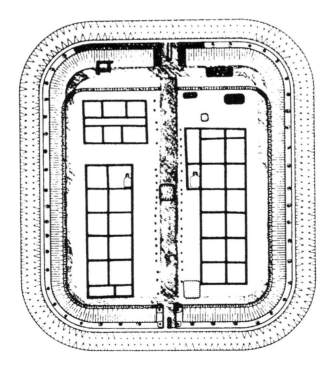

Fig. 64: Haselburg: fortlet. Period 1, A.D. 150–170/80; period 2, A.D. 170/80; period 3, A.D. 170/80–259/68.

This line of tents was faced by another set out in the same way, the two lines together forming a pair or maniple (fig. 65; cf. pl. 27). There is a clear relationship between the size of the centurion's tent and the soldiers' tents: the centurion's tent is twice as wide and twice as deep as the others and the space set aside for the storage of arms and baggage takes up all the remaining space of a rectangle circumscribing the whole. Certain elements of this arrangement are characteristic features of more permanent accommodation (pl. 24). The men's quarters of the barracks are subdivided into rooms (*contubernia*) corresponding to the individual tent-groups, and there is a persistent trend for these *contubernia* to be subdivided into front and rear rooms (pl. 26) corresponding to the area of the tents and that of the space for the weapons in front of them (referred to in much of the academic literature as *papilio* and *arma* respectively—there is no evidence for the ancient use of these terms, although *papilio* was the name given by the Roman army to the *contubernium* tent, after its resemblance to the butterfly chrysalis); the space set aside for baggage and animals may be seen to have been transformed into a veranda fronting the *contubernia* in a line with the front of the centurion's quarters (fig. 66).

Such barrack buildings did not appear ready-made, but were the end product of a fairly swift train of development. Excavations at the Augustan fortress of Oberaden have revealed a series of fairly substantial timber-built centurions' quarters in association with men's accommodation which, while possibly still tented, nevertheless was made more durable by the addition of alternative light timber structures and drainage gullies (fig. 67). Similar evidence comes from the Augustan site of Dangstetten. Further, it has been suggested that the regularly spaced postholes, delineating structures interpreted as barracks at Rödgen, in fact represent the posts of an elaborate timber canopy intended to make the long winter more sustainable in the tents.[3] Such an interpretation is possible, although the structures as envisaged would be prone to instability and lift-off in the manner of an umbrella. Whatever the truth, the buildings at Rödgen can be seen to belong to the first phase of the development of the characteristic Roman army barrack. By the Claudian period, barracks had achieved a recognisable norm of construction.

From the Claudian period until the reforms of Diocletian, the barracks of the Roman Army can be categorised according to a considerable range of 'types', of which two predominate (fig. 68).[4] Type A has officers' quarters which project in front of the line of the men's quarters in the manner outlined above for the tents of Hyginus'

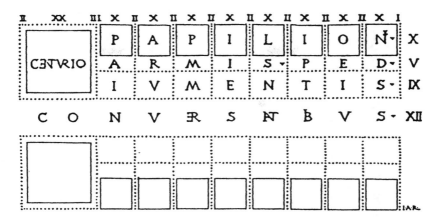

Fig. 65: Tents of a maniple in a marching camp, according to Hyginus.

marching camp; the *contubernia* of the men's quarters are divided into *papilio* and *arma* and the space in front of them may or may not have a roofed veranda. Type B has officers' quarters which do not project in front of the line of the men's quarters, but like Type A it has men's quarters whose *contubernia* are divided into *papilio* and *arma*. Very occasionally a roofed veranda may extend along the front of the barrack. The barracks in the legionary fortresses are almost exclusively of Type A. The barracks in the auxiliary forts are equally divided between Types A and B, and other barrack types form only a very small proportion of the whole.

In spite of having the same basic plan, the size and plan of the barracks varied very considerably; some comparative plans are illustrated in fig. 69 (p. 170). Legionary barracks could, in general, be anything from 30 m to 100 m long, 7 m to 15 m wide; auxiliary barracks from 15 m to 80 m long, 4 m to 13 m wide—though there are examples even beyond these ranges.[5] The largest legionary barracks have an area of c. 1500 m², the smallest of c. 210 m²; the corresponding range for auxiliary barracks is from c. 1040 to c. 60 m². A characteristic overall size for a legionary barrack may be taken to be 80 × 11.5 m and that of an auxiliary barrack to be 48 × 9 m. Variation in the fortlets is too great to make such generalisations useful. There is a clear tendency in the fortress barracks for the centurion's quarters to take some 33 per cent, and in a much smaller number of examples 25 per cent, of the overall

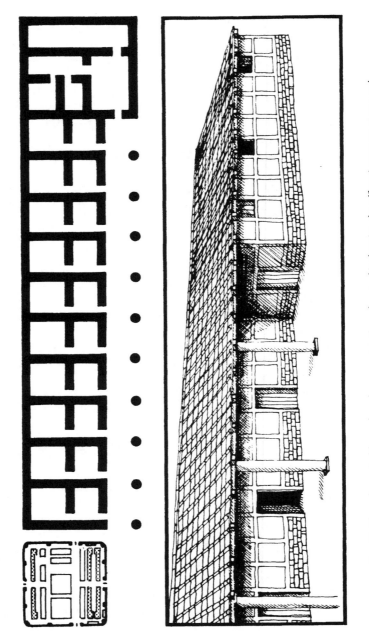

Fig. 66: Plan of a typical barrack and a reconstruction of part of it showing the officers' quarters at one end.

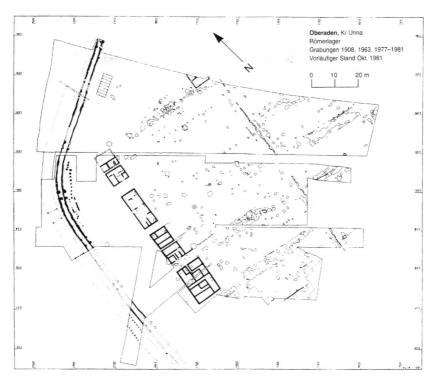

Fig. 67: Oberaden: fort, 11–8/7 B.C. North-west corner, areas under excavation 1977–81.

length of the barrack. In the fort barracks, the same calculation shows a peak at 25 per cent of the overall length, but also a much more general distribution between 20 and 30 per cent of the whole, as well as many others outside this range. This difference in size between the centurions' quarters in the fortresses and the officers' quarters in the forts is one of the most striking differences between the barracks in fortress and fort; it is relatively much greater than that between the men's quarters and clearly relates to the considerable status of the legionary centurion (who on occasion might be placed in command of a small auxiliary unit) as opposed to his auxiliary counterpart.

At their most elaborate, the centurions' quarters in the fortresses take the same form as the courtyard houses described above; but such provision is made only for the centurions of the first (most senior) cohort at Inchtuthil, Caerleon, Nijmegen and Lambaesis, and possibly at

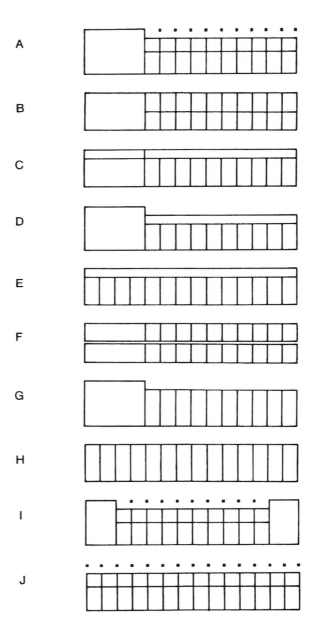

Fig. 68: Barrack types.

Haltern, Lauriacum and Carnuntum. This reflects the great importance of these senior centurions; indeed the *primus pilus*, or senior centurion of sixty carefully ranked centurions, stood immediately below the senior tribune in the fortress hierarchy of command and received a grant on discharge from service sufficient to acquire equestrian status. The quarters of most legionary centurions are rather simpler buildings, although still very large (pl. 25). The arrangement of their rooms takes many forms and probably reflects the wishes of their first occupants. In general the plan resembles that of Roman town houses with a series of rooms opening off a longitudinal corridor. In the auxiliary forts, the relatively small size of the officers' quarters did not usually allow any particular architectural form, but were simply subdivided into a number of small rooms. The centurion's quarters were usually integral with the rest of the building, but sometimes they were divided by a narrow alley or passage some 2m wide. Given the size of the centurion's quarters, the passage would have greatly facilitated movement about the fortress. The same feature is very occasionally found in auxiliary forts.

The numbers of *contubernia* in the legionary barracks vary between ten and thirteen; those in the auxiliary barracks have two major concentrations on eight and ten but additionally occur frequently over the whole range from six to eleven. It has often been claimed that these variations reflect the different theoretical strengths of the various types of auxiliary unit; comparison of all the evidence does not bear out this theory.[6]

The internal areas of the single *contubernia* in the legionary fortresses concentrate between 20 and 25m^2; those in the auxiliary forts range rather more widely between 15 and 27m^2. Given that eight men formed the complement of the *contubernium*, it can be seen that the allocation of space per man, in contrast to the centurions'/officers' quarters, is not greatly different between the fortress and the fort, about 2.85 as against 2.5m^2. But this calculation has many complicating factors. It is not possible to know the extent to which the *contubernia* were occupied by their proper complement of eight; indeed cavalry *contubernia* may have had a complement of six. The eighty-man strength of the legionary century may have been distributed throughout the eleven or twelve *contubernia* and both legionary and auxiliary units may have been over or under titular strength; further, the barracks may, or may not, have been built to meet those circumstances. In all situations the barracks may have been built merely to fill available space on the ground rather than according to a theoretical space per man allocation

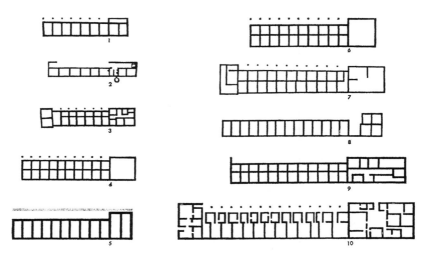

Fig. 69: Comparative plans of barracks in Roman forts and fortresses: (1) Hesselbach, period 2; (2) Hod Hill; (3) Valkenburg, period 1; (4) Fendoch; (5) Housesteads; (6) Künzing; (7) Echzell; (8) Haltern; (9) Caerleon; (10) Lambaesis. Scale 1:1550.

(in spite of the strict gradations between different units stated by Hyginus). Nevertheless the similarity in size of the basic *contubernium* unit between the fortress and fort is noteworthy.

The proportion of the *contubernium* taken by the *papilio* in the legionary fortresses concentrates between 61 and 67 per cent of the whole; in the auxiliary fort the entire range between 40 and 73 per cent is almost evenly represented, but a marked peak is found on the point of 50 per cent which is almost totally absent in the fortresses. While most of the legionary barracks have *contubernia* of the same size and form throughout their length, there is a substantial minority where the first (next to the centurion's quarters) and last *contubernia* are different in size and form; such special *contubernia* are found only exceptionally in the barracks in auxiliary forts and fortlets. Various explanations may be presented for the form of these special *contubernia*, but the very variety of the different types tends to deny a single simple interpretation, and excavation has failed to reveal any clear answers. The first *contubernium* may perhaps have been a guardroom or storeroom, possibly for the artillery equipment of the century. On occasion it seems to have acted as an entrance hall to the centurion's quarters, but this is not an arrangement which is demanded by the layout of most centurions' quarters.

Bogaers and Haalebos have suggested that the special first *contubernia* at Nijmegen may have been the location of the foot of a staircase leading to a second storey.[7] The most plausible explanation for the special end *contubernia* is that they provide more extensive accommodation for the *principales*, or NCOs, of the century who would number at least three: *tesserarius*, *optio* and *signifer*. Where special end *contubernia* occur, the irregular nature of their internal divisions suggest that they were used for accommodation rather than stores, although other examples devoid of internal divisions are also known and are best interpreted as stores.

The above may be taken to be a summary of the composition of the barracks. It should be remembered that in every fortress and fort there were very considerable variations between individual barrack buildings (no matter how uniform they may initially appear in plan) and that the apparent uniformity of the buildings tends to obscure a considerable lack of knowledge and understanding of their structure and function; indeed some basic questions concerning the architectural form of the barracks must be addressed.

The veranda with *porticus* is a feature of the barracks of the auxiliary forts (pl. 30), but one which is much less pervasive than in the legionary fortresses. Type A barracks have the form most suitable for the inclusion of a *porticus* (and thereby the creation of very considerable loft space) in the design, but there is a considerable number of barracks of this type where clear evidence for the *porticus* is lacking. Examination of the dimensions of these particular barracks suggests that when the officers' quarters extend too far from the line of the men's quarters, the covered veranda is omitted. This in turn implies the possibility that in these barracks (and in others) the roof line of the officers' quarters lies at right angles to that of the men's quarters, or at least is of separate and independent construction; in those barracks with a *porticus* the roof line is likely to continue in the same alignment for the whole length of the barrack. It is no surprise that in all barracks where there is no veranda, there is a strong trend for the *arma* to take up a greater proportion of the whole *contubernium*; in particular the 1:1 proportion is that most often found in Type B barracks. This implies a building of much simpler construction, as illustrated in fig. 69.

Most barracks were self-contained structures and can reasonably be imagined to have had simple pitched roofs. There is, however, a substantial number of barracks, particularly in fortresses but also in forts, which are built with a party rear wall. This conformation renders the access of light to the *papiliones* very difficult without the construction of some kind of clerestory, and it is thus that most of the reconstructions are drawn. This however raises problems: if there is a clerestory, either the *papilio* must be considerably higher than it is broad or deep, and furthermore would lose all heat up into the roof, or we must imagine it with a ceiling, in which case the clerestory becomes pointless except to lighten a second-floor room. The presence of such rooms would tend to obviate the need for the clearly delineated *papilio* and *arma* whose presence is such a persistent feature of the legionary barracks and of most of the auxiliary barracks. It seems more probable that admission of daylight to the *papiliones* in those barracks with party rear walls was not considered very important. There is no shortage of finds of lamps in the barracks. Twin ridges are the most likely form of roof construction; rainwater could easily be drained by means of central timber guttering (fig. 70). It may be added that the uniformity of the size and depth of barrack wall foundations gives no reason to suggest that some supported clerestory or even second-storey superstructures.

If there is doubt over the form of various elements of the barracks, their manner of construction is better known. It may be assumed that the legionaries constructed their own principal buildings and barracks. *RIB* 334 records such work at Caerleon, where the legionaries of *II Augusta* restored from ground level the barracks of the seventh cohort. The inscription can be dated between A.D. 255 and 260. The identity of the builders of the barracks in auxiliary forts is by no means so certain. The only inscription specifically to refer to this records that work was carried out at Bainbridge by the *Cohors VI Nerviorum*; the date of the inscription is A.D. 205.[8] The epigraphic evidence shows that construction work on auxiliary fort defences and principal buildings was carried out predominantly by legionaries until the second half of the second century, after which point operations were increasingly taken over by the auxiliaries themselves. It is true that stone inscriptions refer only to stone forts and that no definite conclusions can be drawn for the earlier earth and timber forts, but it would seem most likely that legionary troops were predominantly responsible for their construction.

Unfortunately this evidence does not answer the question of who built the auxiliary barracks. It is reasonable to assume that the auxiliaries built their own barracks, at least from the time when they were mainly responsible for the major internal buildings; but before that date it can only be an assumption. On the other hand, if the legionaries were occupied with the defences and major buildings, the construction of their own barracks would be a task which the auxiliary garrison could usefully perform. The contrast in the standard of construction of the barracks at Newstead Period 3 (Antonine) between those of the legionaries in the *praetentura* and those of the auxiliaries in the *retentura* suggests precisely this process.[9] Both kinds of troops had built their own barracks.

The layout of all the buildings clearly related to the detailed architectural conception of the fort or fortress. Much attention has recently been drawn to the possible use of standard units of measurement in Roman military construction;[9] the question, however, is fraught

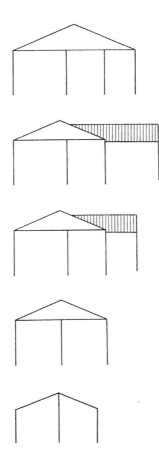

Fig. 70: Roof construction.

with problems, and there are so many variables that it becomes very difficult to distinguish intended dimensions, particularly when small measurements are in question, for example the breadth of a *contubernium*. In fact the great majority of barrack dimensions shows no direct relationship to units of Roman feet, and the discrepancies suggest that the barracks themselves were not intended to be of particular dimensions, but rather were being built to fill the space available between the streets, rather than according to pre-ordained dimensions to satisfy *per capita* space allocation. This can be seen in those fortresses where the outline of the defences is highly irregular, as at Vindonissa or Carnuntum, where the barracks were of different lengths throughout the fortress. Possibly even more telling is the variation usually found between the lengths of the individual barracks even in a rectangular cohort-block, for example at Inchtuthil.

If it is imagined that the barracks were laid out according to pacing by centurions, it is easy to see that the dimensions will vary from any theoretical norm. Such a procedure would make it a simple matter to set out the barrack in any particular proportions, and would also make it easy to use the breadth of a *contubernium* as a multiple in the composition of the whole barrack.[11] Such can be seen in the barracks at Neuss and Bonn where the breadth of the *contubernium* divides into the length of the centurions' quarters seven times. It must again be stressed that such relationships can only occasionally be clearly seen, and less in the barracks of the auxiliary forts than in the legionary fortresses.

Thorough site preparation was the prelude to all building activity in fortress, fort and fortlet. Having been drained and cleared, the site was levelled and all natural depressions filled. Only very rarely were sites terraced or buildings erected on sloping ground. Clay was often used for levelling and, on re-used fort sites, it was common practice to cover the remains of any former fort with a thick layer of clay. It is likely that tents provided the first accommodation for the men on most sites, both legionary and auxiliary, as first the officers' quarters were completed and then the rest of the barrack. Tell-tale indicators such as small postholes are often noted, as are possible drainage trenches and channels. Tent pegs often provide more direct evidence.

Nearly all the buildings were built of some form of timber framework which could be constructed according to a number of different techniques. The most simple of these was to set the main timber uprights into individual post-pits about 1.30 m deep and 0.60 m in diameter. The most careful examples show the placing of a base-plate in the form of a flat stone at the foot of the post; often this is interpreted as legionary work. Post-trench construction was the technique most often used for timber buildings. Trenches some 0.30 m wide and 0.40 m deep were dug, into which timber uprights were placed at intervals and the earth backfilled. The uprights were not pointed, but had flat bases. In section they could be round, rectangular or square. Most examples show the use of all these types in the same building with the stronger being placed at the most important points. Typically the posts were 0.18 m square or in diameter with spacing of about 1 m. In many instances the construction was highly systematic; just as often it was very haphazard. Timber ground sills occur less frequently, but are not uncommon. Their rigid platform would have been particularly well suited to coping with unstable ground conditions. Ground sills were usually placed in a construction trench, but this did not need to be as deep or wide as the post-trenches; on the other hand the trench needed to be level and straight and therefore this technique was unsuited to very difficult ground. It is possible, also, that sometimes the sill beams were placed directly on top of the ground surface.[12]

The vulnerability of the wooden uprights to rot must have been a principal factor which led to their replacement by stone sill walls. In most of the frontier provinces stone-sill construction in the fortresses began in the Claudian/Neronian period; in Britannia it is rather a feature of the Trajanic/Hadrianic period. In auxiliary forts and fortlets the picture is different. The major buildings of the fort, of which the *praetorium* was one, were constructed with stone sill walls before the barracks and other buildings, but in general it may be said that stone-sill construction again begins in Britannia in the Trajanic/Hadrianic period; however, outside Britannia, stone-sill construction is essentially a feature of the Antonine or even the Severan period. It seems likely that the construction of barracks entirely in stone was very rare, although the major buildings may more commonly have been so constructed; it is difficult to be certain when so little of the above-ground evidence survives. Where it does appear, it is a feature of the late Roman period.

On top of the sill walls a timber superstructure would have been built as before, usually with a sill beam as a base. The foundation trenches for the walls were typically 0.70 m deep and 0.80 m wide. Usually they were filled with broken stones or cobbles and bonded with clay. The use of mortar in the foundations was very unusual. The width of the sill walls was rather less than that of the foundations and ranges from 0.40 m to 1.00 m; 0.70 m was typical. The standard height of the walls cannot be known, but at Neuss the height of the sill wall corresponded to one-third of the breadth of the foundation and they were sealed on top with a layer of tiles.[13] This gives a height of about 0.30 m. The sill walls themselves usually consisted of stones whose faces were roughly dressed and set in clay with a clay and rubble core. The lowest one or two courses were often given a greater overall width than those above. Again the use of mortar in construction was highly unusual.

The superstructure of the walls was nearly always of wattle and daub construction. Horizontal wattling (*opus craticium*) was more common than vertical wattling. Narrow upright staves intervened between the main uprights and the ends of the wattles were fitted into slots in the uprights. Horizontal wattling was clearly the form best suited to walls with stone sills. The walls themselves were wider than their foundation trenches and the daub completely enclosed the uprights and framing. Weatherboarding may occasionally have been added to the walls, but the usual protection took the form of a lime wash or plaster. Sometimes the plaster consisted of little more than a wash, but it was often more sophisticated and consisted of several graded layers. Peters considers that the walls of the barracks at Nijmegen were plastered and whitewashed inside and out, and this must probably be regarded as the norm, although there are instances where such plastering was clearly lacking, for example at Longthorpe.[14]

Finds of painted plaster deriving from the barracks are quite common in fortresses, although rather less so in forts and fortlets. Furthermore, within the barracks, provision was usually greater for the centurions' and officers' quarters than for the men's. The most extensive evidence has come from Nijmegen, and Peters' conclusion is that although it is possible that some of the most elaborate wall-painting in the fortress came from the barracks, it is more probable that the centurions' quarters had simple panel decorations while the men's quarters had white walls with red socles.[15] More elaborate decoration is found in the centurions' quarters in many other fortresses; the designs include floral decoration allied to concentric circles, polychrome geometric patterning and figural representations. The most dramatic example of wall-painting has been found in the *triclinium* of the officers' quarters of a barrack at the auxiliary fort of Echzell in the Taunus, where three picture fields were represented in an architectural framework depicting Theseus and the Minotaur, Daedalus and Icarus, and Fortuna and Hercules, with accompanying wreaths of flowers and black and white grapes.[16] The standard of the painting was of good workmanship and clearly is highly unlikely to have been carried out by the residents. In all these instances the painting was applied *al secco* on top of a fine lime wash.

Tiles provided by far the most common form of roofing; alternatively occasional use was made of local materials: slates, stone, shingling and thatch. The occurrence of runnels formed by the dripping of rainwater along both sides of the barracks suggests that they usually had a simple pitched roof; this is confirmed by the fairly common find of eavesdrip guttering fashioned from half logs for timber barracks. Barracks with stone sill walls often had eavesdrips formed of dressed stone. Roof guttering has been found (for example at Oberaden), but its presence is exceptional. The most usual supports for the veranda roof were wooden posts established in postholes; also common were stone bases into which a socket had been cut for the upright. Barracks with stone sill walls also often provided bases of similar construction for the uprights. Stone columns are known but exceptional. Apart from simple pounded earth, the most usual veranda flooring was of cobbles, although stone flags and timber flooring are also known.

The internal flooring of the barracks took a great variety of forms: pounded earth, clay, sand, stone paving (pl. 28), masonry chippings, broken chalk, gravel, light cobbling, broken tile. It is likely that timber flooring was more common than many excavations have revealed; light cobbling or gravel would form a good foundation for timber joists. Concrete floors were also common, often combined with crushed tile to form *opus signinum*. More sophisticated were tessellated floors composed of small tesserae of tile; and mosaic floors have also occasionally been found. It should be noted that flooring varied much within individual barracks. In general *opus signinum*, tessellated and mosaic floors are more often found in officers' quarters and in legionary barracks.

The doors to the *contubernia* were some 0.90–1.00 m wide and were usually supported on pivots rather than hinges. Window glass is often found in the vicinity of the barracks indicating common usage. The height of the windows cannot be known, but plaster remains from the auxiliary fort of Echzell indicate a fairly high position for them, that is with their bottom edge some 2m from the ground level.[17] The remains of hearths are often found in the *contubernia* and it is probable that they were a standard feature in most barracks. Heating was their primary purpose, but cooking was probably also an important subsidiary role.

They are most commonly found in the *papilio*, built up against the middle of the dividing wall from the *arma*. Thus positioned under the highest point of the roof, they would be well placed either for a chimney or for some smoke outlet in the roof if there were no ceiling. Hearths are also often found in the officers' quarters. Often they are situated in one of the small rooms at the very end of the barrack; these rooms thus may be interpreted as kitchens. They are also to be found heating one or more of the living rooms. There is a substantial minority of barracks where no traces of hearths have been found. It is likely that braziers formed the alternative source of warmth and cheer in these instances. Hypocausts are virtually unknown in the barracks. The most notable exception is that found in the quarters of the *primus pilus* at Inchtuthil, especially unusual in a timber building. A further example occurs in the quarters of one of the centurions of the first cohort at Caerleon, this time a building with stone foundations. Small versions of this kind of heating system are to be seen in the areas mainly of the centurions' quarters at Lauriacum and Carnuntum and are to be dated to the end of the third century and later.

Officers' quarters were often provided with small latrines which were usually located in one of the small rooms at the end of the quarters in order to have access to the fortress or fort drains running past the ends of the barracks. Such rooms often had tiled or stone floors sloping in the direction of a small drain which in turn connected with the main drain. When there were no drains, cesspits sufficed. The latrines were often associated with washing facilities which were contrived to provide some flushing action. Small baths in the form of shallow basins some 1.5 m square are sometimes found. Latrines have been found in almost every possible position in the men's quarters. The end of the veranda was a fairly usual location; very often also a whole *contubernium* would be given over to a latrine emplacement. Cesspits, soak-aways and bucket emplacements are all found.

Storage pits of various kinds have been found in all parts of the barracks. The most elaborate are best described as cellars and these are most often found in the officers' quarters. The most impressive to have been found is one of two at Hofheim (Erdlager). It measured 11.5 × 3.0 m, was provided with steps and lined with timber and must have had a timber cover. Inside were found at least five amphorae.[18] Such pits were often filled with rubbish on the evacuation of the fortress or fort, but there were other pits whose primary purpose was the reception of rubbish. Small regular pits are often found along the line of the veranda in front of the *contubernia*; these would have been appropriate for small flat-bottomed buckets or baskets and subject to regular emptying.

Little is known of the furnishing of the *contubernia*. The most obvious arrangement would be to have four sets of bunk beds in the *papilio* ranged round the hearth; but this would sometimes not be possible in the space available. In the *papiliones* at Heidenheim Cichy found numbers of small postholes which he interpreted as the remains left by bunks against the rear and side walls and by small tables in front of the hearths.[19] Very few traces of any such arrangement have survived elsewhere (nor would they in many modern barracks). In the absence of other evidence it must be assumed that the more common practice was for the men to sleep on palliasses which could be tidied away during the day if necessary; that is in spite of the difficulties of stepping over recumbent bodies in the middle of the night.

The presence of so many substantial hearths in the *contubernia* raises the question of whether they were used for cooking. Finds of the necessary large cooking vessels are almost unknown; on the other hand graffiti show that each *contubernium* had its own crockery and mess utensils, furthermore that a small hand-mill may well have been part of the normal equipment of the *contubernium*. These small mills could have been used to prepare oats and pulses for biscuits or soups cooked in the *contubernium*. Bread stamps and the frequent provision of one oven per barrack (cf. pl. 26) in fortresses and forts imply that the organisation of the bread supply was based on the *centuria* or *turma*.

Sufficient cook-houses have also been identified to suggest that the principal catering provision was centralised, but it must be likely that animals which were the product of the chase (or of purchase in the *uici*) such as hare, wood pigeon, game birds and fish were cooked at the *contubernium* hearth. The soldiers in fortresses, forts and fortlets made use of both fine tablewares and local native wares as well as coloured glass plates, bowls and drinking vessels. There is a greater wealth of deposit in the centurions' and officers' quarters, but finds derive from all parts of the barracks.

A wide variety of semi-official duties must have taken place in the *contubernia*. Equipment had to be cleaned, repaired and even made. Traces of metal working and leather working are often found. The barracks too had to be cleaned. The duty roster of *Legio III Cyrenaica* gives a day's duty for one of the thirty-six men of a century as 'sweeper in barracks' (*scoparius*), while C. Aemilius Valens had to work on the uniform of Helius on the second and third days, and on the ninth day

P. Clodius Secundus had to clean Helius' boots.[20] No doubt Helius was the centurion.

The finds of inkwells bear witness to reading and writing activity in the barracks, but there is little doubt that games of chance were more popular pastimes. Gaming counters and evidence for board-games come from almost every military site. All this took place very often in the presence of votive dedications. Small altars dedicated perhaps to the 'genius of the century', to the legion's standard-bearers, or to the Mother Goddess are occasional occupants of the barracks.[21]

It remains difficult to get to the truth of barrack life. There were considerable contrasts in the provision made for the officers in the fortress on the one hand, and for the officers in the fort and fortlet on the other, while the distance between officers and men is clear in all circumstances. In comparison, much less pronounced is the discrepancy between the men's quarters in fortress and fort. Certainly the centurions and decurions in the auxiliary barracks often had amenities which were lacking in the *contubernia* of the legionary barracks. This is as true in the first century as in the third, and is all the more striking in view of the non-citizen status of the auxiliaries. The finds of quality table service and in particular of glass vessels from all parts of the barracks witness life of some quality with the opportunity for the exercise of taste, and yet the inevitably rather cramped conditions and the limited washing facilities suggest that life was sometimes rather squalid. At least it is possible to accept Professor Robertson's succinct appraisal of the life of the soldiers at Castledykes: 'The garrison ate meat from oxen and pigs, used glass bottles and lived in timber and clay barracks'.[22]

NOTES

1. The tablets found there include correspondence of the commandant's wife; and there are children's shoes among the finds. See A.K. Bowman, *Life and Letters on the Roman Frontier* (London 1994), 57.

2. [Hyginus], *Liber de munitionibus castrorum*, 1.

3. See J.-M.A.W. Morel's article 'Tents or barracks?' in *Roman Frontier Studies 1989*, ed. V.A. Maxfield and M.J. Dobson (Exeter 1991).

4. D.P. Davison, *The Barracks of the Roman Army from the 1st to 3rd Centuries A.D.* (Oxford, 1989), 4f. and fig. A on p. 267.

5. For a diagram showing graphically the range of sizes of barracks and other buildings, see Davison, op. cit., fig. 2 on p. 281.

6. Davison, op. cit., 12f.

7. In *Hakoerier* (1983), 10–11.

8. *Journal of Roman Studies* 51 (1960), 192f.

9. Report of the 1947 excavations by I.A. Richmond in *Proceedings of the Society of Antiquaries of Scotland* 84 (1949–50), 1–38.

10. Detailed discussion by C.V. Walthew, 'Possible Standard Units of Measurement in Roman Military Planning', *Britannia* 12 (1981), 15–35.

11. Ibid., 22–23.

12. For a notable example of this type of construction, compare the Hadrianic 'palace' at Vindolanda (above, Chapter 4, p. 112).

13. C. Koenen, 'Novaesium', *Bonner Jahrbücher* 111/112 (1904), 97–242.

14. Nijmegen: W.J.T. Peters in *Berichten van de Rijksdienst voor het Oudheidkundig Bodemonderzoek (in Nederland)* 29 (1979), 373–402. Longthorpe: S.S. Frere and J.K. St. Joseph 'The Roman Fortress at Longthorpe', *Britannia* 5 (1974), 1–129.

15. Peters, ibid., 379.

16. Personal communication from D. Baatz.

17. Personal communication from D. Baatz.

18. E. Ritterling in *Nassauische Annalen* 34 (1913), 67.

19. B. Cichy, *Das römische Heidenheim* (Heidenheim 1971), 27f; also in *Denkmalpflege Baden-Württemberg* 1 (1972), 33–38.

20. R.O. Fink, *Roman Military Records on Papyrus* (Cleveland 1971), 108–10. More accessibly in G.R. Watson, *The Roman Soldier* (London 1969), 222–31.

21. Dedications to the 'Genius of the Century' were found in the vicinity of barracks at Vindobona and the Saalburg. At Chester there was an inscription to the Genius of the standard-bearers of *legio XX Valeria Victrix* (*RIB* 451). A possible *sacellum* to Mother Goddesses was excavated in a barrack of the Roman fort of the *Classis Britannica* at Dover (*Britannia* 8 [1977], 424; 426f).

22. *The Roman Fort at Castledykes* (Edinburgh/London 1964), 264.

Glossary

agora (Gk), the central open space in a Greek town, often its market-place (cf. *forum*)

alae (lit. 'wings'), the spaces, or open-fronted rooms, on either side of the *atrium* or *tablinum*

ambulatio, a terrace for walking, open or covered

andron (Gk 'men's apartment'), a corridor connecting the *atrium* with rooms behind

apodyterium, the changing-room in a suite of baths

apse, a semicircular recess in the wall of a building

arma, an equipment area in front of a military tent; the front room of a *contubernium* (q.v.)

arx, a citadel

atrium, the main central hall of a *domus* (q.v.); for the different types, see pp. 38ff

aula, a reception hall; (in palaces) a throne room

basilica, a rectangular (usually aisled) hall

caldarium, the hot room in a suite of baths

castellum, (in water supply) a tank receiving water from an aqueduct and distributing it to properties

cenatio, a dining-room (see also *triclinium*)

civitas, an organised community, a city with its surrounding territory; in Britain and Gaul, a tribe, its administrative centre being referred to by modern writers as the '*civitas* capital'

colonnade, a row of columns, usually fronting a covered walk

column, a post, normally circular in section, supporting an entablature (q.v.)

compluvium, the rectangular opening in the middle of the inward-sloping roof of an *atrium* (q.v.)

contubernium, a tent-group of eight men, and the rooms accommodating them in an army barrack

cornice, the topmost part of an entablature (q.v.), immediately below the roof

cryptoporticus (Gk *kryptos* 'hidden'), a closed passage or gallery, sometimes with windows

cubiculum, a bedroom; extended to denote other private rooms

diaeta (Gk *diaita* 'abode'), a room (Lat. *cubiculum*), esp. an open rest room

dome, the hemispherical roof of a circular or polygonal room or building

domus, a private house (esp. in a town), forming a self-contained unit

entablature, in trabeated (q.v.) construction, the horizontal members above the columns

exedra (Gk), an open recess or alcove with seats

fauces (lit. 'throat'), the entrance passage leading from the street to an *atrium*

forum, the main central square of a Roman town; a market-place (e.g. *Forum Boarium,* the cattle market at Rome)

frigidarium, the cold room in a suite of baths

gymnasium, a centre for physical training; in general, esp. in Greek lands, a school

hortus, a garden; in plural (*horti*), a suburban estate

impluvium, the shallow rectangular basin in the middle of the floor of an *atrium*

insula (lit. 'island'), (1) originally, a tenement or apartment block, usually several storeys high; (2) in modern usage, an area in a town bounded by streets: see discussion, p. 3

kepotaphion (Gk), a tomb-garden

lararium, a shrine of household gods (*Lares*)

mansio, a rest-house, providing accommodation for travellers on official business

nymphaeum (Gk *nymphaion*), an ornamental fountain

oculus, an opening at the top of a dome

oecus (Gk *oikos* 'house'): a reception room opening off a peristyle

opus, a method of construction or style of decoration: *opus craticium*, trellis-work; *opus sectile*, floor or wall decoration of coloured marble panels cut to shape; *opus signinum*, flooring of crushed tile mixed with concrete

palaestra (Gk *palaistra* 'wrestling-school'), an exercise ground, often attached to public baths

palatium, (1) originally, the Palatine hill in Rome; (2) the Imperial Palace there; (3) by extension, any imperial residence

papilio, a military eight-man tent; the rear room of a *contubernium* (q.v.)

paradeisos (Gk), the parkland of an eastern king or noble

peristylium (Gk *peristylon*), a peristyle, an open courtyard or garden surrounded by colonnades

pilaster, a square pillar partly projecting from a wall

piscina, a fish-pond, or pool in general

porticus, a portico or colonnade

posticum, a door at the rear of a house

praetentura, the forward part of a military establishment

praetorium, (1) the official residence of the commander of a military base; (2) hence, a large official (or even private) residence

principia, the headquarters building of a Roman military base

puteal, a well-head

retentura, the rearward part of a military establishment

salutatio, a Roman noble's formal morning reception of his clients

taberna, a shop

tablinum, a large room at the back of the *atrium*

tepidarium, the warm room in a suite of baths

tetrastyle, having four columns

topiarius (Gk *topos* 'place'), a landscape architect, an exponent of *ars topiaria*, 'place-art'

trabeated (Lat. *trabs* 'beam'), the constructional technique of the classical Orders, in which columns support horizontal beams (opposed to 'arcuated', using arches or vaults)

triclinium (Gk *triklinon*), a dining-room, properly one with couches on three sides of a central table

triconchos (Gk *konche* 'shell', hence 'apse'), (a room) with three curved recesses

vault, an arched roof covering a passage or room

vestibulum, an entrance porch

villa, a country house, normally part of a working farm, usually divided into *pars urbana*, the residential quarters, and *pars rustica*, the farm buildings

viridiarium, a conservatory or flower-bed, a place for *viridia* 'green things'

Guide to Further Reading

The most recent general book in English on this topic is by A.G. McKay, *Houses, Villas and Palaces in the Roman World* (London 1975). The sections on housing in A. Boëthius, *Etruscan and Early Roman Architecture* (Harmondsworth 1978) and in J.B. Ward-Perkins, *Roman Imperial Architecture* (Harmondsworth 1981) should also be consulted.

The author of our Chapter 1 has written a book on town planning in the classical period: E.J. Owens, *The City in the Greek and Roman World* (London 1991). Still useful is J.B. Ward-Perkins, *Cities of Ancient Greece and Italy* (London 1974). Both these should be consulted for the planning of residential areas.

On houses in the country, John Percival, *The Roman Villa* (2nd edition, London 1988) is the standard work and enlarges on the matters he discusses in Chapter 2.

For further information on town houses, palaces and gardens it is best to go to guides and other books on the individual sites. M. Grant, *Cities of Vesuvius* (London 1971) is a good introduction to Pompeii and Herculaneum. There are detailed discussions of the interior decoration, mainly of town houses, in J.R. Clarke, *The Houses of Roman Italy, 100 B.C.–A.D. 250* (Berkeley 1991); and on their gardens see W. Jashemski, *The Gardens of Pompeii* (New Rochelle NY 1979). There is a comprehensive treatment of Ostia in R. Meiggs, *Roman Ostia* (2nd edition, Oxford 1973). The palaces of Nero and Domitian in Rome are fully discussed by W.L. MacDonald, *The Architecture of the Roman Empire I* (New Haven 1982). The Italian archaeological guide books published by Laterza, Milan, are excellent and frequently updated, though individual entries are sometimes brief: those by F. Coarelli on *Roma* (1980) and *Lazio* (1982) are particularly good.

Many other reports and discussions of individual sites are listed in the footnotes to each chapter. On military housing, see the book by the author of Chapter 6: D.P. Davison, *The Barracks of the Roman Army from the 1st to 3rd Centuries A.D.* (Oxford 1989); also the following:

D.J. Breeze, *Roman Forts in Britain* (Aylesbury 1983)
P.A. Holder, *The Roman Army in Britain* (London 1982)
A. Johnson, *Roman Forts of the 1st and 2nd Centuries A.D. in Britain and the German Provinces* (London 1983)
L. Keppie, *The Making of the Roman Army* (London 1984)
G. Webster, *The Roman Imperial Army* (London 1969)
R.J.A. Wilson, *Roman Forts* (London 1980).

Index of Sites and Buildings

(NOTE—All sites are listed under their ancient name where this is known, with cross-reference from the modern name if this differs significantly. The numbers against the names of sites provide a key to the maps. Certain sites, which are not mentioned in the main text, are indexed by reference to the illustration or note in which they appear.)

Map I: The Roman World, West

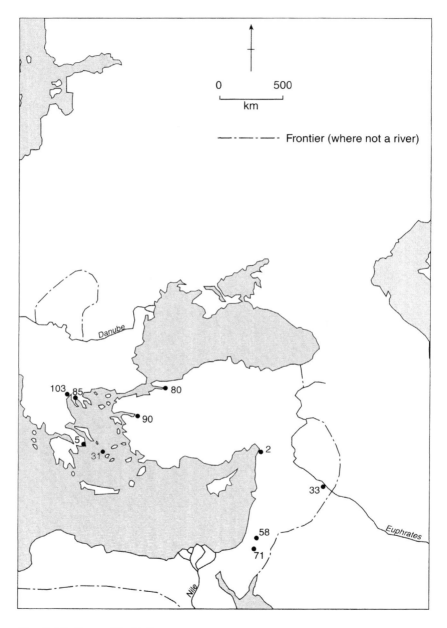

Map II: The Roman World, East

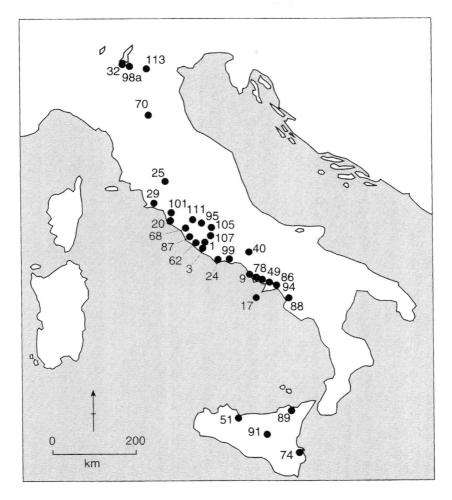

Map III: Italy

Map IV: Roman Britain